envisioning writing

To my good friends,
Mary Ann and Frank

Jan

ENVISIONING WRITING

TOWARD AN INTEGRATION OF DRAWING AND WRITING

Janet L. Olson

HEINEMANN
PORTSMOUTH, NH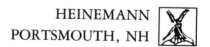

HEINEMANN EDUCATIONAL BOOKS, INC.
361 Hanover Street   Portsmouth, NH 03801
Offices and agents throughout the world

The following have generously given permission to use quotations from copyrighted work:

Figure 4-1: From *A Study of Writing* by Ignace J. Gelb. Copyright 1952. Published by The University of Chicago Press. Reprinted by permission.

Every effort has been made to contact the copyright holders and the students for permission to reprint borrowed material. We regret any oversights that may have occurred and would be happy to rectify them in future printings of this work.

Library of Congress Cataloging-in-Publication Data
Olson, Janet L.
     Envisioning writing : toward an integration of drawing and writing/
Janet L. Olson.
        p.   cm.
     Includes bibliographical references and index.
     ISBN 0-435-08700-2
     1. Visual learning—United States.   2. Art—Study and teaching
(Elementary)—United States.   3. Language arts (Elementary)—United
States.   4. Drawing—United States.   5. English language—
Composition and exercises—Study and teaching (Elementary)—United
States.   6. Special education—United States.   7. Verbal learning—
United States.   I. Title.
LB1068.O47   1992
372.6′044—dc20   92-7322
                                                             CIP

Designed by Wladislaw Finne.
Printed in the United States of America.
92 93 94 95 96   9 8 7 6 5 4 3 2 1

To Alan, Maren, Sonja, Irving, and Olive

A picture is a fact.

—LUDWIG WITTGENSTEIN

contents

acknowledgments

There are many to thank regarding the research and publication of this book. First, I would like to thank David W. Baker, who has seen this project develop through many stages. As the director of art for the Brookline Public Schools, he supported and facilitated the beginning of my research. After becoming the program coordinator for art and art education at Teachers College, Columbia University, he acted as the chairman of my dissertation committee. Without his encouragement, this book would never have become a reality. I would like to thank the other members of my dissertation committee: Irving Kaufman, art educator; Dorothy S. Strickland, language-arts specialist; and Margaret Jo Shepherd, specialist for the learning disabled. Their respective insights and expertise were invaluable to the refining of my work.

I would also like to thank Brent and Marjorie Wilson of Pennsylvania State University. It was their research on narrative drawing that became the impetus for my own research in the Brookline Public Schools.

I also wish to thank Pat Ruane, Sy Yesner, and Naomi Gordon, who included me in discussions, committees, and presentations related to the teaching of writing in the Brookline Public Schools. Their support gave me a great deal of confidence to proceed.

The students, parents, teachers, and the principal(s) of the Edith C. Baker Elementary School in Brookline, Massachusetts, also deserve special thanks. Being an art specialist for sixteen years at this remarkable school was truly a privilege.

Although hundreds of students provided me with "insights" supporting the thesis of this book, a special thank you is due to the following students whose work is included as specific examples: Steven Alzamora, Delores Avery, Andy Berman, Steven Berman, Alycia Cavadi, Gabrielle Chodes, Evan Cohen, Kevin Curry, John Driscoll, Rusty Feldman, Karen Fried, Robert Ginsberg, David Goldberg, Kojo

Griffen, Dan Harrington, Shawn Harris, Christine Hennessey, Cora Horsley, Richard Iannessa, Tom Kelleher, Chris Kelley, Gerald Knight, Joyce Kodsi, Steven Lander, Lisa Lenthal, Aaron Levine, Jonathan Levine, Adi Loebl, Cyndy Lyons, Christine Mahoney, Bill McDermott, Paul McKinlay, Angel Moncrieffe, Jonathan Morales, Kate Novak, Raisin O'Regan, Jonathan Parial, Melissa Park, Alessandra Pogglio, Jeffrey Price, Sonja Reid, Nicole Rolbin, Gil Rosenthal, Sharon Rutman, Paul Scheinkopf, Billy Simmons, Sam Simon, Ina Stith, Tor Strom, Larry Sugarman, Liz Uretsky, Connie Villalba, Debra Wasserman, Adam Weinstein, Rachel Weinstein, Barrie Wheeler, Richard Wheeler, Danny Yee, and Peter Zalkalus.

Finally I would like to thank my husband, Alan. Without his love, support, and encouragement, I would have, most likely, given up this project a long time ago. There were many times when he had more faith in my work and ability than I did. He truly believed that I had something important to say and he generously gave of himself in order to support me in my effort.

INTRODUCTION TO THE PROBLEM

VISUAL OR VERBAL LEARNER?

Many children have problems with language. Is it because they are "learning disabled" or "reluctant writers"? Or is it because they aren't being taught the way they need to be taught? Children who think and learn visually process information through images instead of through words, and these children often have great difficulties succeeding in school. My classroom observations, made over a twenty-year period, suggest that such children are in danger—they don't progress well academically, they perform poorly on tests, and they often suffer from poor self-esteem.

Children who think and learn verbally, on the other hand, are best served by the present teaching methods in the public schools. Teachers, especially in the language arts, are verbal in their behavior and training, are expected to be so, and expect their students to be or become so in turn. Whether the language arts are taught by conventional or innovative methods of instruction, words are used to elicit more words. An examination of any language-arts curriculum and/or text such as Moffet (1968), Carroll and Chall (1975), or Calkins (1986), will reinforce that this is the case. In such a setting, the visual learner is left out.

And yet the drawings of these children indicate that they see the world in great detail. They do not think that it's necessary or even desirable to say in words what is clearly seen and known in images. This book shows that by a process of "envisioning" writing, visual learners do, in fact, improve their writing skills.

In describing how visual and verbal children process information, Dixon (1983) refers to a study by Clementina Kuhlman, and he states:

> Verbal children tend to do well on tasks that require a sensitivity to the conventional, culturally understood, functional qualities of things. For example a ball, a balloon, and a hula hoop would be linked together on the basis that they are toys. Visual-spatial children, on the other hand, tend to associate things on the basis of recognizing patterns in their physical qualities. The ball, balloon, and hula hoop would be associated on the basis of being round. One could say that verbal children are culturally sensitive, while spatial children are physically sensitive. Verbal children do

well when conventional understanding is important, while spatial children do well when being aware of physical properties and patterns in things is important. (57–58)

Why haven't art educators previously brought this problem to light? Quite simply, art educators have been much more concerned with the "child artist" than with the "child learner." In other words, if language-arts educators have been blind to visual children, art educators have been deaf to their language difficulties. Indeed, art teachers should understand visual learners best of all (even though, unfortunately, this is not always true); they need to realize that children with highly visual aptitudes are capable of complex problem-solving and thinking processes. Unless these children learn to communicate their thinking with words, they will not be fully understood or appreciated throughout the school community and will, in fact, never achieve their full educational potential. It is the art teacher's responsibility to educate the school community as to the strengths and weaknesses of the visual learner. Only when art educators systematically assume the comprehensive responsibility for educating children will the visual arts be viewed as offering a necessary and essential part of every child's education. In other words, when the relationship between visual literacy and verbal literacy is understood and the results of a visual-narrative program are clearly established, the visual arts will finally be viewed as having equal status with the language arts and no longer be viewed as a "frill" to be victimized by budget considerations again and again. Art educators, in short, have perceived their instructional roles much too narrowly, as Arnheim (1969) has also argued:

> The discipline of intelligent vision cannot be confined to the art studio; it can succeed only if the visual sense is not blunted and confused in other areas of the curriculum. To try to establish an island of visual literacy in an ocean of blindness is ultimately self-defeating. Visual thinking is indivisible. (307)

Art educators need to broaden their perspective to include a genuine concern for the total education of the visual learner. If language arts has been guilty of overemphasizing words as a method of instruction, the visual arts have been equally guilty of not emphasizing words enough. Feldman (1971) seems to understand this:

In order to cope with the world, you have to be able to translate from one language to another—from or to a visual language, a kinetic language, an aural language, an oral language. You have to be able to translate what you see into what you say and do. (118)

Many visual people think that everyone sees the way they see and are surprised to find out that this is not the case. And many highly verbal, nonvisual people think that visual people are deficient when they can't immediately understand the meaning of others' talk or express themselves accordingly. Visual learners, while being quite aware of the high priority placed on verbal skills, are rarely rewarded because their efforts fall short of what is expected. It is not surprising, then, that they frequently become "ever-more-reluctant" writers, readers, and speakers. Ben Shahn describes this difficulty in the following way:

It is sometimes very difficult for me who most often thinks in images rather than in ideas. I have occasionally done magazine illustrations, and I bring them in to the editor, who is essentially a word man. And until I have surrounded the image that I have brought in with certain words, he does not get it. Then suddenly some word helps him to get it. He needs that bridge apparently. But my own habit is naturally to think in images. (Morse, 1972, 44)

We might assume from this explanation that most visual people in our society are artists. But Vera John-Steiner (1985) reports that physicists, biologists, mathematicians, and engineers are also highly inclined to be visual learners. She suggests that the artist and the scientist go about their work in a similar way:

Of greatest importance in the thought activity of artists and scientists is their pulling together of ideas, images, disarrayed facts and fragments of experience, which have previously been apprehended by them as separated in time and space, into an integrated work. (77)

Indeed, J. C. Gowan reports that "in the case of every historic scientific discovery which was researched carefully enough, we find it was imagery, either in dreams or in a waking state, which produced the break-through" (John-Steiner, 1985, 87). John-Steiner concludes that this process is the essence of creative thought.

The critical question, then, is to what extent are visual learners being adequately served by general educational practice? How can visual learners be identified, and what problems do they face in schools today? Why are so many of these children identified as being learning disabled? What are the biases and misunderstandings held by specialists in language arts, art education, and special education? And how can we change this educational problem into an instructional opportunity?

We must begin by confronting the almost universal belief held by teachers that visual expression is separate from verbal expression. While many of us recognize and support the values that make up art-education curricula, we fail to understand what is actually involved with visual thinking. Arnheim (1969) explains this type of thinking as follows:

> My contention is that the cognitive operations called thinking are not the privilege of mental processes above and beyond perception but the essential ingredients of perception itself. I am referring to such operations as active exploration, selection, grasping of essentials, simplification, abstraction, analysis and synthesis, completion, correction, comparison, problem solving, as well as combining, separating, putting in context. These operations are not the prerogative of any one mental function; they are the manner in which the minds of both man and animal treat cognitive material at any level. There is no basic difference in this respect between what happens when a person looks at the world directly and when he sits with his eyes closed and "thinks." (13)

The visual expressions of students are rarely, if ever, acknowledged as a form of language that can be questioned, explored, interpreted, and translated into other modes of expression. Visual learners are given no way to improve their verbal language skills. Albert Einstein (1976) explains this process very well:

The words or the language, as they are written or spoken, do not seem to play any role in my mechanism of thought. The physical entities which seem to serve as elements in thought are certain signs and more or less clear images which can be "voluntarily" reproduced and combined.

The above-mentioned elements are, in my case, of visual and some muscular type. Conventional words or other signs have to be sought for laboriously only in a secondary stage, when the mentioned associative play is sufficiently established and can be reproduced at will. (142)

Einstein's understanding of himself as a visual thinker is further explained by Susanne Langer (1942): "The limits of language are not the last limits of experience, and things inaccessible to language may have their own forms of conception, that is to say, their own symbolic devices" (265). John Updike (1963) describes this same process through one of his characters as follows:

He saw art—between drawing and writing he ignorantly made no distinction—as a method of riding a thin pencil line out of Shillington, out of time altogether, into an infinity of unseen and even unborn hearts. He pictured this infinity as radiant. How innocent! (185)

Teachers, while they might appreciate this nondistinction coming from Updike, must also come to see this kind of thinking and learning among their students. It is a well-documented fact that 15 percent or more of all children do not respond well to verbal instruction (Taylor, 1979, 214), and many more children have varying degrees of difficulty with it. A value chart could be used to visualize these many variations (see Figure I–1). If white represents visual learners and black represents verbal learners, it's easy to see how many variations of gray are possible within the two extremes. The children who respond poorly to verbal instruction may very well be the children who simply cannot or will

Figure I–1

*Visual and verbal
value chart*

not pay attention, who will not lead or participate in class discussions, who seem unable or unwilling to follow directions, and who are very likely to be classified as being daydreamers, discipline problems, learning disabled, or all of the above.

These children do indeed have a very real learning disability in the public-school context. They may be handicapped by finding themselves in a disabling environment, one that is too narrow to serve and enhance their visual aptitudes. As Sattler (1982) puts it in a cartoon depicting a psychiatrist's analysis of a teacher lying on a couch: " 'Your feelings of insecurity seem to have started when Mary Lou Gurnblatt said, "Maybe I don't have a learning disability—maybe you have a teaching disability" ' " (398).

Nothing is wrong with children who are visual learners. They are simply different from verbal learners. Teachers need to understand and incorporate visual thinking and visual learning strategies into conventional teaching methods in order to make it possible for both types of learners to reach their full language potential. Obviously, this should be the common goal for art, language-arts, and special-education teachers. But it is a realizable goal only if we begin to recognize that it is the instructional process that needs correction—not the child.

Drawing and writing need to be integrated in our schools. This book shows how it can be done. Visual and verbal modes of learning can indeed be woven together in the classroom. Language need not and should not be separated from its initial visual component—this way, *all* types of learners can benefit.

The book is divided into two parts. Part I, "Toward a New Methodology: Envisioning Writing and Educational Practice," shows a variety of specific teaching strategies and activities appropriate to visual-arts, language-arts, and special-education classrooms. The need for new strategies becomes blatantly clear after viewing the children's art and reading their narratives. They speak strongly and convincingly for themselves.

Part II, "Theoretical Implications for Visual and Verbal Learners," presents two sources for understanding why the visual learner is not well served in educational practice today. History is considered first. Important and relevant clues are found in the development of language and in previous educational theories and practices related to the teaching of writing. Secondly, current educational goals, beliefs, and practices employed in the fields of art education, language-arts education, and special education are considered. By closely comparing them, we will gain a fuller understanding of both their similarities and their differences. If their common goals are understood, we can emphasize their similarities rather than their differences for the sake of the learner. With this theoretical framework, educators interested in deepening their understanding of the methods suggested here will be able to continue developing more of their own teaching strategies.

TOWARD A NEW METHODOLOGY: ENVISIONING WRITING AND EDUCATIONAL PRACTICE

CHAPTER 1

THE ART-EDUCATION PROGRAM

If we are at all concerned for the child as *learner* as well as the child as *artist*, we must include visual-narrative drawing in our art curricula. Visual-narrative drawing provides a natural basis for both visual and verbal literacy, with neither being sacrificed for the sake of the other. In fact, both will become stronger, since each naturally informs the other.

The foundation for this book was a visual-narrative drawing program that began during the 1977–1978 academic year at the Edith C. Baker Elementary School in Brookline, Massachusetts. At that time, professors Brent and Marjorie Wilson of Pennsylvania State University were employed as art-education consultants for the Art Department of the Brookline Public Schools. The Wilsons (1979a) believed that children have a natural but largely unexplored inclination to tell stories with their drawings. Unfortunately, this natural inclination in children remains generally unexplored—traditional programs in art education have never devoted much time to exploring the narrative dimension of children's artwork. Yet the Wilsons maintained that if children are encouraged to develop and explore their "private visual worlds," we may be able to understand the nature and meaning of this unique kind of cognitive activity more fully. If visual thinking can be understood and accepted, then it should be possible to develop an entire art curriculum based upon the drawing of visual stories. The purpose of the visual-narrative art curriculum that I designed (Olson and Wilson, 1979) was to develop the visual-narrative drawing skills of children further by stressing the storytelling components of character, setting, plot, and even special effects. When students' drawing skills improved, so did their visual vocabulary. They were able to draw more detailed, more complex, and more satisfying stories. And it is by attending to their own stories, according to the Wilsons (1982, 104), that children create whatever is appropriate to their own needs and concerns. It is through the very structures of story that plot, character, and consciousness are integrated (Bruner, 1986). This is why Bruno Bettelheim (1977) defends the pedagogical value of fairy tales in the face of those who would argue that many fairy tales expose children to unpleasant and even terrifying images and that, therefore, such stories should be avoided. To the contrary, Bettelheim argues, it is "just because life is often bewildering" that such tales must be used responsibly, for "the child needs even more to be given the chance to understand himself in this complex world with which he must learn to cope" (5).

Drawing plots for the imaginative world of fantasy and fairy tales is particularly powerful—and with good reason. The visual capabilities of some children are much more highly developed than their verbal, prosaic, and analytical capabilities. This is why fantasy and fairy tales translate so well out of verbal narratives into the world of visual imagery, whether by illustrations, comics, or film animations, for it is the translation into the visual that places a premium on immediacy. The visual-narrative approach to writing takes advantage of these properties by acknowledging that the elements of plot are frequently more complex and detailed in children's drawings than is evident in their writings.

Can children's interest in drawing stories be sustained throughout an entire year? The answer is yes. The Wilsons' theories concerning children's natural inclination to tell stories with their drawings were confirmed at the Edith C. Baker Elementary School. It is indeed possible, from the foundation of visual-narrative drawing, to address and evolve all the other, more traditional, artistic concerns such as use of materials, techniques, composition, elements and principles of design, as well as traditional concerns for art history, criticism, and aesthetics.

A NEW METHODOLOGY

Characters   One way to begin teaching through visual narrative is to ask students to fill a piece of 12″ × 18″ drawing paper with as many different kinds of people as they can think of (see Figure 1–1). A short discussion stimulates their imagination and gets them started. Ask students how many different kinds of people they can name and also encourage them to think of the visual clues that distinguish them from another kind of person. They will name "fireman," "policeman," "ballerina," "baseball player," "grandpa," "baby," "teacher," "caveman," "spaceman," "witch," and many, many more. This kind of sharing can easily be made into a game by using teams or by compiling private lists to be shared later. Or students could take turns around the room giving examples. If they can't name a different kind of person, they are "out,"

Figure 1–1

Different kinds of people

and the winner is the last one remaining. By the time they run out of possibilities, they will have so many ideas for their drawings they may even ask for multiple sheets of drawing paper.

New characters can also be developed following a discussion on exaggeration (see Figure 1–2). The class can brainstorm answers to "How many ways can a person be exaggerated?" Suggestions will be, "too tall," "too fat," "too skinny," "too pretty," "too ugly," "too mean," and so on. Students can again fill a sheet of 12″ × 18″ drawing paper with their ideas. Exaggeration can also be suggested following an observational drawing lesson (see Figure 1–3). After drawing a classmate, students can be asked to imagine how their classmate would look if he were too tall, too skinny, too short, too fat, and so on.

When children discover they have access to so many possible characters, they will no longer rely on a limited number of simple stereotypical characters. They will become more visually aware, searching for the visual clues that will distinguish their unique characters.

Art teachers should be particularly observant when their students are drawing their characters. When they move around the room they will see a great deal of thinking taking place. Many students will begin drawing their characters doing something. This is important, for the introduction of action signals the first or initial stage of the narrative dimension of meaning. Some students become so deeply involved with the narrative dimension of their drawing that they begin to provide sound effects to accompany the drawing. Their characters speak with a variety of voices, their machines chug, toot, clang, and roar as the action zooms and crashes! These sounds may expand into highly complex dialogues between characters. Some students will begin to introduce props into their drawings, meaning something in addition to the character, such as a fire truck, hose, or a burning building drawn near a fireman (see Figure 1–4). Props permit the expansion of narrative detail. They also provide a reason for the location of the character and provide a sequence of meaning.

Teachers should continue to work on character development. Students need to be exposed to a wealth of possibilities, such as "How

Figure 1–2

Exaggerated people

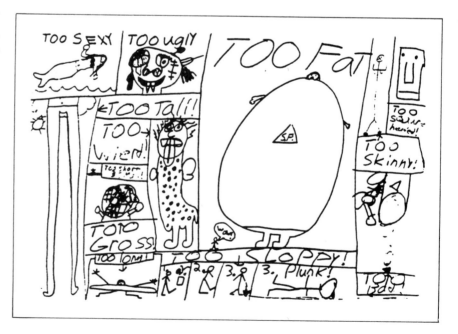

Figure 1–3

Observational drawing and two exaggerated drawings of a classmate

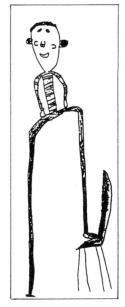

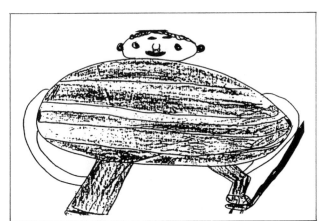

Figure 1–4

Characters with props

many kinds of bugs can you draw? Dogs? Animals? Cars? Space creatures?" and so forth.

Once students have developed a collection of character drawings, the narrative possibilities increase dramatically. Through the process of drawing, students will already have well-developed plans for their characters. Their plans will consider the abilities and the limitations of their characters, based on the occupation, age, and/or a unique physical or personality characteristic of the character (such as "too fat," "too tall," or "too sad"). These special characteristics will be considered further as their characters continue to develop.

Movement Students love to bring their characters to life by introducing movement (see Figure 1–5). Making characters move requires practice and careful observation. When students don't know how to draw a particular movement, they should carefully observe a classmate who simulates the movement. Students should observe and practice drawing characters who run, jump, bend, climb, reach, pull, dance, walk, and so forth. This is a problem-solving activity and, as much as possible, should be discovered through observation by the students. They are learning to "see." The teacher's role at this time is to ask leading questions, which can lead to the necessary discovery and solution. Examples of leading questions could be

- How could you show that he is walking *slowly*?
- How could you show that he is running very *fast*?
- What parts of his body bend when he picks up a ball from the ground?
- What happens to her head when she is dancing?

Teachers should think of themselves as facilitators in this problem-solving process. Observation from life is just one avenue to a possible solution. The art room should be filled with resources for students to use in search of an acceptable solution to their particular problem. A large variety of art books, reproductions, magazines, photographs, picture books, and the like makes it possible for students to see how artists throughout history have solved similar problems. For example, Duchamp's *Nude Descending a Staircase*, Matisse's *Dance*, and Chagall's

Figure 1–5

Characters moving

Birthday each solve the problem of movement in quite different ways. Children need to know that they can solve visual problems in a variety of ways.

Students who think that they cannot bring characters to life through movement soon discover that it isn't as difficult as they once thought. When the art teacher encourages a wide variety of solutions to any given visual problem, stressing visual communication rather than rendering a realistic, representational drawing, the anxiety of not being able to accomplish the task is greatly reduced. The pressure to make or the impossibility of making the so-called best drawing is no longer a factor, and drawing can again fulfill its most primary and basic function—communication!

Emotions   When characters can dance, fall, run, and climb, they can easily begin to relate to one another. And this can be accomplished more effectively if these characters can show a variety of emotions and feelings (see Figure 1–6). The ability to show characters who cry, who are frightened, who are happy or angry, will make it possible to develop even more interesting and detailed visual stories.

As students begin to draw characters depicting specific emotions, it will soon be noticed that in some cases the so-called "good artist" will be able to draw an attractive, stylized face and yet be unable to make that face manifest a variety of different feelings. This is ample testimony for avoiding a formula for drawing faces, for the student can be trapped within such formulaic designs that it becomes very difficult to experiment with a wide range of possibilities for showing emotions. Through discussion and observation (as in the case of drawing movement), the narrative drawing skills of children will improve greatly with respect to their ability to depict emotion. A few questions that could be asked are

- How do your eyes change when you are afraid or surprised?
- What happens to your eyebrows?
- Does your mouth change when you are angry?
- When do you get lines in your forehead?

Such questions, and many more, can provoke intense and serious inquiry as students make various faces for one another or study their

Figure 1–6

Emotions and feelings

own faces in a mirror. Students will become aware that it is more than the mouth that changes when the emotions change.

Fantasy   A child's imagination is a wonderful resource for a wide range of characters. Many children never seem to run out of ideas, as demonstrated by two sixth-grade boys who took black magic markers and a roll of white shelf paper home with them. After spending a few hours after school together, they returned the next day with a ten-foot

Figure 1–7   drawing filled with a wide range of fantasy characters (see Figure 1–7). I got the impression that they had not run out of ideas, but had simply

Ten-foot drawing of fantasy characters

run out of time. Other students need a little help to exercise and stretch their imaginations. Again, it can be very helpful for children to carefully observe the fantasy drawings of professionals, such as the illustrations by Brian Froud and Alan Lee (1978) for their book *Faeries*. Several of their fantasy characters were photographed with slide film and projected so an entire class could observe the detail simultaneously. The students did quick sketches in an effort to capture the essence of each character (see Figure 1–8). It is the art teacher's responsibility to draw students' attention to important details they may have overlooked by occasionally asking a leading question, causing them to focus on a particular detail. For example:

Figure 1–8

Fantasy characters inspired by illustrations by B. Froud and A. Lee

• Did you notice how long his stringy hair is?
• Did you notice how close together his eyes are?
• Did you notice that big hump on his back?

Whether or not students actually include every detail in their own drawings is not as important as whether they are able to capture the essence of the character. Capturing the essence of an image requires selective visual observation. By carefully observing the fantasy drawings of others, children gradually build a store of reference material they can call upon when they draw their own imaginative characters.

Relationship   Relationships between characters are obviously very important elements in a story. One must know, for example, whether the characters are similar in age or whether there are great differences. An art teacher can introduce this subject by simply asking, "How do people change as they grow older?" and "What are the visual clues that help you determine how old a person is?" (see Figure 1–9). Discussion will include clothing, interests, physical abilities, and physical characteristics such as size, posture, and skin textures. Students should also be encouraged to look for examples from reference materials such as those mentioned earlier.

The relationships between characters are also influenced by their proximity to one another. The space between characters becomes an important element in a visual story.

Settings   A well-thought-out visual setting can provide a great deal of information for the viewer. If a setting is not provided, children will often ask one another, "Where are they?" for characters have to be somewhere! Stories can take place indoors, outdoors, or a combination of both, but that is just the beginning step when planning a setting. There are many elements to consider when planning a setting for a story, and the art teacher should help to broaden the students' view of what is possible in order to expand their visual vocabulary.

If the story takes place indoors, for example, the point of view is important. The student might draw a room as though he is looking down from the ceiling and can see all the furniture as well as the arrangement of objects on top of tables, desks, and bureaus (see Figure

Figure 1–9

How people change as
they grow older

1–10). Or the setting could be drawn as though the viewer is looking straight into a room (see Figure 1–11). This view makes it easier to see what is on the walls of the room, including windows and doors. A story might also be told from the point of view of something in the room such as a mouse or a spider. In each case, the story will dictate what point of view is most appropriate to the setting, but these elements, in turn, will have a lot to do in determining how the story develops.

The art teacher helps the student consider details that will assist the narrative dimension of the story by asking questions such as:

- What time of day is it? What clues could you include to make it clear?
- Are the characters who live in this house rich or poor, old or young?
- Is the time of the year important to know, and if so, how could you show that?

When raising questions of clarification, the teacher should always be careful not to dictate a solution. The purpose of questioning is to set up a problem and to leave the student with choices for the solution. For example, "night" could be indicated by a lighted lamp, a person sleeping, a moon through a window, the time on a clock, as well as many other possibilities. Teachers are facilitators. They should introduce a wide range of considerations and possibilities, but the student should always have the right to accept the question as valid and important to the story, or reject it as an unnecessary consideration. Students are generally eager to please and are trained in most other subject areas to get the "right" answer, so if the art teacher offers only one suggestion to a problem, the student will most likely accept it as "best" and not search for or consider other more creative solutions. For example, if the teacher suggests drawing a Christmas tree in a room to indicate winter, the student may not consider other possibilities, such as a fire in the fireplace, snow falling on leafless trees outside a window, boots sitting by the door, and so on. Obviously, too much detail or information can sometimes be distracting and unessential, but the student should always be in control of the story. Art teachers should simply nurture the creative process.

Changes in the outdoor environment can also be a very convenient

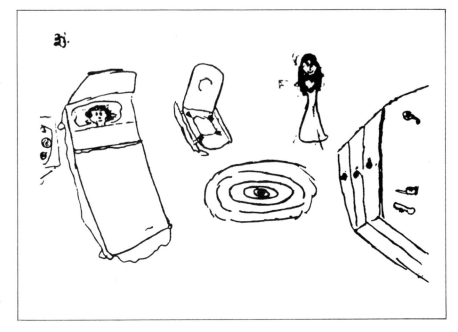

Figure 1–10

A room drawn from above, looking down from the ceiling

Figure 1–11

A room drawn from the front, looking in

vehicle when telling a visual story (see Figures 1–12, 1–13, and 1–14). In order to generate thinking on the range of possibilities, the art teacher could begin by asking, "How many ways can the outside change?" Students will suggest changes in temperature, weather, seasons, and the like. They will provide a seemingly endless list of visual details that could be included, such as lightning, dark clouds, rain, bent trees, wind, birds, flowers, and so on. The discussion could become more focused if the teacher sets up specific situations. For example, asking how changes in weather could affect a picture of a boat in the middle of the ocean, a car being driven through the countryside, or a crowded city. This would also be a good time to introduce works of art in order to familiarize students with how well-known artists have solved similar problems. Some examples could be Hopper's *Ground Swell*, Chagall's *Snowing*, Homer's *The Gulf Stream*, Van Gogh's *The Starry Night*, or Munch's *White Night*.

The art teacher can also expand this discussion and introduce the element of fantasy in planning settings. Obviously, the possibilities are endless. Works by Dali, Magritte, Rousseau, Chagall, Ernst, and Tanguy would be good references for this discussion.

Plots If children are able to draw a variety of characters, make them move, change their emotions, as well as control a variety of changing environments, they then have access to a rich visual vocabulary that will serve them well when developing an interesting and meaningful plot. In order to develop a plot for a visual story, children must be able to depict a sequence of events. Putting events into a logical order is not an easy task for many children. There are numerous ways to give children practice in sequencing. What follows is a description of just three of the many possibilities.

Literature as a Resource In order to facilitate the development of personal "dream stories," we used Maurice Sendak's *Where the Wild Things Are* (1963) in one class. Sendak's book is highly visual, with only a minimal use of words to support the plot. Many pages have no words at all. The plot is simple, but has universal appeal for children, which explains its enormous success. The story is about Max, a little boy who has been very naughty. His mother calls him a "wild thing" and sends him to his

Figure 1–12

Changes in the outdoor environment

Figure 1–13

A day

Figure 1–14

A year

room without any supper. Max crawls into bed and soon begins to dream. Leaving home, he gets into a small boat and sails away to an island where the "wild things" live. Max encounters big, scary monsters but is ultimately able to tame them. They like Max. But Max gets lonesome and chooses to go home. When he wakes up, he is relieved and happy to be in his safe and secure little room. This feeling of security is reinforced when he sees a warm supper waiting for him on a table in the corner.

Children love this story and don't mind seeing and hearing it repeatedly. They are eager to describe their own dreams and nightmares, whether they are funny, strange, fantastic, or even terrifying. They talk about how some people dream frequently, while others don't seem to remember dreaming at all.

The students are then instructed to draw a sequence of pictures based on one of their own dreams, each on a separate piece of 9″ × 12″ drawing paper. If they want to change the plot a little to make the dream funnier, more fantastic, or scarier, they should be encouraged to do so. The number of drawings depends on the length of the dream, and the students can include words where they feel they are necessary. The students finish their very own "dream-story" books by making a title page (including a picture, a title, and the student's name) and then stapling all the pages together (see Figure 1–15).

Music as a Resource Since music is naturally sequential, it provides excellent motivation for a visual-narrative sequence. Music that has definite changes in mood or tempo works particularly well. "In the Hall of the Mountain King" from the *Peer Gynt Suite* by Edvard Grieg is a good example of music that can suggest a wide range of imagery. The first step is to listen to the music very carefully. I tell students that if they listen very carefully, they will hear the movement of the little trolls who live in the mountains. I also remind them of the fantasy creatures they drew earlier while observing the drawings by Brian Froud and Alan Lee in their book *Faeries*. I note the visual similarities between their creatures and trolls. Teachers may also refer to the classic children's story *Three Billy Goats Gruff*, probably the most well-known story featuring a troll character. Because this music is being used to inspire visual interpretation and sequential imagery, rather than to study

Figure 1–15

A dream-story sequence

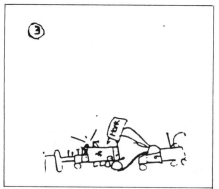

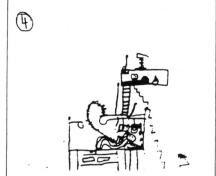

Grieg's already existing plot, the story of *Peer Gynt* need not be introduced. After discussing trolls, the students will be eager to listen to the music for a second time. They may want to listen for changes in the music. They will discover that the music is composed of three very distinct and unique parts: a slow plodding beginning; an active and very busy middle; and a loud, crashing ending. The music may need to be played a couple more times to ensure that each student can distinguish the three parts. Then, the most important question needs to be asked: "What do you think *could* be happening?" Keeping the beginning, the middle, and the end of the musical piece in mind, the students will offer a wealth of possibilities. Some of their suggestions include dramatic weather changes, the construction of buildings, and enemy invasions. A couple of suggestions may even be role-played by small groups of students.

Finally, the students plan their own interpretations by drawing a triptych, a sequence of three pictures (see Figures 1–16 and 1–17).

Figure 1–16

A triptych inspired by Edvard Grieg's "In the hall of the Mountain King"

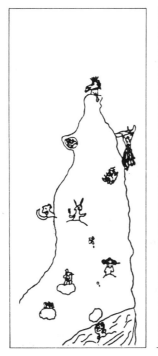  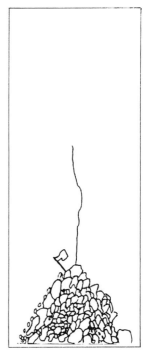

Figure 1–17

*A second triptych
inspired by Grieg*

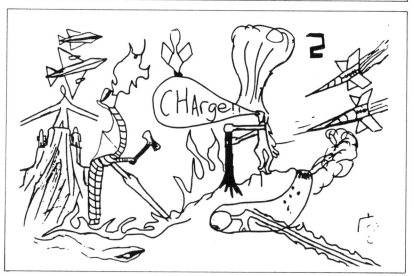

*Works of Art
as a Resource*

Narrative drawing is a wonderful way to put children in touch with the history of art. Edmund Feldman's method of introducing children to great works of art is the first step (Olson, 1982). It is Feldman's notion that children can be taught to appreciate the great works of art by talking about them. Feldman, somewhat like Socrates, uses a unique question-and-answer approach that elicits from even very young children "what they see" in a given painting (1981, 466–84). Unlike Socrates, however, he does not have a preconceived notion as to "what" they must eventually see. His approach is designed instead to make children comfortable with verbalization and to view it as a process of discovery. When young children are permitted to become personally involved by talking about the narrative content of a work of art, their attention span is amazingly long. One begins by selecting works of art that have good narrative content, such as works by Bearden, Shahn, Magritte, Goya, Hopper, Degas, Rembrandt, Vermeer, Bellows, and Wood. The following is a description of a lesson beginning with the study of Grant Wood's *American Gothic*.

Using Feldman's method of inquiry, the discussion begins with the question, "What do you see in this picture?" The children then take turns naming everything they can see, beginning with the largest and most obvious images. They move systematically from the obvious two main figures and the building in the background to the task of naming and describing every detail of the painting—the man's glasses, his clothes, the flower-print dress of the woman, and so on. This process continues until it becomes a competitive and challenging game to see a detail in the picture that no one else has seen. The students' eyes become absorbed, searching for one more minute detail. The students are then asked leading questions about the couple and the setting, such as "What do you think he does for a living?" "How does she seem to feel?" and "Where do you think they live?" Their answers must be based on clues from within the painting, such as "He must be a farmer because he's holding a pitchfork," and "She must be mad at him because she's scowling," and so forth.

Following this very detailed discussion, the students are then asked to make their own drawing of *American Gothic*, trying to be as accurate as they can. Although this is a controversial issue, many art educators such as Brent Wilson, Al Hurwitz and Majorie Wilson (1987) believe that children learn a great deal from the classical approach of visual imitation. The children will pay close attention to the smallest detail, and yet the childlike quality of their drawings will not be lost (see Figure 1–18).

By now the children have an enormous amount of information about this painting. They are now ready to use their imaginations in a visual-

Figure 1–18

Drawings inspired by Grant Wood's American Gothic

narrative exercise. By posing questions such as "After Grant Wood painted this picture, what do you think happened?" or "What did the man and woman do next?" teachers can encourage students to share a wide range of possibilities, with nothing being too far out! Some of the scenarios will be plausible and others will be fantastic, such as imagining that the couple got into their spacecraft and went to the moon for a vacation!

After sharing many of their ideas, the children will be ready and eager to draw their own stories (see Figure 1–19).

Figure 1–19

Visual narrative inspired by Grant Wood's American Gothic

Special Effects   Some children are always interested in doing something a little different or unusual when they create a story and special effects can fascinate them. Drawing people, buildings, or other objects from a strange point of view can add drama or even humor to a story (see Figure 1–20).

Drawing a gradual transformation or metamorphosis creates another kind of special effect (see Figure 1–21). A person changing into an animal, a shoe changing into a car, or a parakeet changing into a puddle could be an interesting development in a narrative. The use of close-ups or "zoom" techniques draws attention to a particular aspect of the story. A well-placed close-up makes sure the viewer sees something that is very important (see Figure 1–22).

Figure 1–20

―――――――――

*Drawing from an
unusual point of view*

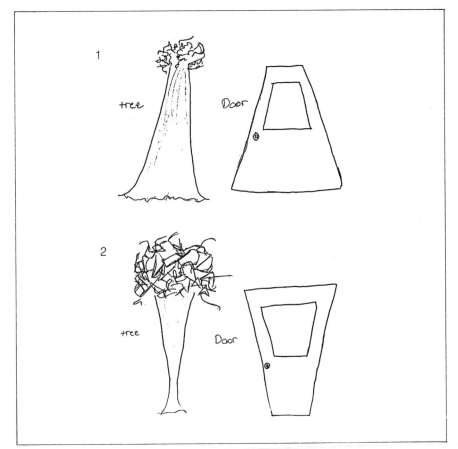

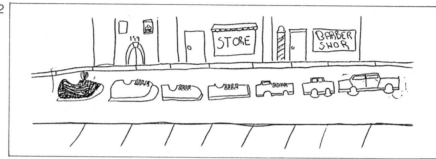

Figure 1–21

A metamorphosis

Children usually enjoy figuring out special effects, and they even invent many of their own. They will get ideas for their drawings from movies, television, and their own personal experiences.

Becoming Informed   Once we're convinced that children use their drawings to tell stories, the enormous wealth of detailed information that they include in them becomes obvious to us. The degree to which a child's drawing is fully

Figure 1–22

Close-up sequences

cognitive appears to go far beyond what most adults are yet able to comprehend or are willing to acknowledge.

The key to becoming an informed teacher and comprehending this uniquely rich form of communication, however, is being sensitive to the child's "ways of worldmaking" (Goodman, 1978). Teachers must first admit that they are not all-knowing—they simply cannot see or completely understand all that is known and communicated in a child's drawing. Consequently, they must first convey to the child a sincere interest and respect for both the child and the artwork, by engaging the child in honest dialogue. Only through this process can a more complete and accurate translation of the work be achieved. This is also the crucial step for learning how what is known visually can inform verbal communication. All children can benefit from this practice, but for those children who are visual learners, it is absolutely essential that they have as many of these dialogical opportunities as possible. For this process to be successful, the teacher must learn to ask the right questions and, above all, to be a very good listener. Only then will teachers become aware of the wealth of information that exists in a child's drawing.

Too often children have the opportunity to share the content of their drawings only with one another. But an entirely new level of awareness and understanding can be achieved if the art teacher takes the time and puts forth the effort to understand the narrative dimension of a child's drawing. Teachers often forget that drawing is the most basic and direct form of visual communication, and too often they glance quickly at a drawing and assume that they have seen and understood everything that is there. This approach does not show much respect for either the work or the child. Art teachers generally judge children's drawings much too narrowly, primarily by the dictates of aesthetics or in relation to how closely the drawing meets adult criteria such as advanced technical skill, realism, modeling, perspective, and the like. This is not to suggest that teachers shouldn't recognize the child who can render a beautifully stylized object or person, but the first step toward these higher goals is to understand the child as communicator. This takes some time, effort, and sensitivity on the part of the teacher.

When children discuss their drawings, the dialogue that develops will serve another very important purpose—it will give them practice translating their visual thinking into the verbal mode. Children who communicate most effectively with visual images assume others already know and understand all that is in their drawing. Very often they make this assumption in order to avoid verbal expression as much as possible by saying, when asked to do so, that they can't think of anything to say or write. But once they begin to translate their own drawings, they also begin to become more comfortable with the verbal mode, because they are operating from a position of strength, a sense of ownership. They know that they are the primary authority when they are discussing their own drawing. The art teacher, in this instance, has to serve as the facilitator of the translation process instead of being an authority regarding what is to be translated. For example, open questions of inquiry should replace statements of fact. "How does he feel?" rather than "He looks sad." "Why is he sad?" rather than "He must be sad because he lost something." "Why did you use dark colors?" rather than "It must be night time." And so on. Students are eager to please and will often agree with a teacher's interpretation rather than present a conflicting one. Consequently, the original intention would be lost.

No part of a dialogical process can be taken for granted, since this is the step that is so critical and sometimes terrifying to children who are visual learners. Verbalizing does not come naturally to them, and it should be the art teacher's responsibility to introduce them to this process in a gentle and nonthreatening way.

SUMMARY

The improvement of visual-narrative drawing skills should be an ongoing process of development and a primary goal of art educators. These skills enable children to communicate more effectively through their drawings; in fact, communication becomes the primary purpose and the driving force behind them. Children are more eager and effective problem solvers if they feel the real need to communicate an idea. For example, if it is essential to the telling of a story that a student be able to draw a lion stalking his prey, that student is likely to be much more willing to do some research on the subject and to plan carefully that particular image. But if the drawing lesson is merely assigned in the abstract—that is, if it has no narrative significance—the student will be little motivated to accomplish this task. The narrative dimension provides the occasion for challenge towards visual communication, and when there is this linkage, a dramatic improvement in visual language often results.

CHAPTER 2

THE LANGUAGE-ARTS PROGRAM

Volumes have been written on the teaching of writing. Every writing methodology has its advocates and its detractors, and there are always those who search for or await the discovery of a way to resolve all issues once and for all. Each new generation of educators criticizes the previous one for failing to recognize the essential ingredients for success. They argue that grammar, spelling, punctuation, and phonics are emphasized too much or not enough, that it's the writing process rather than the finished product that is important, that free expression is what really counts, or that formal rules of grammar and composition are being neglected. Television is sometimes blamed as being the cause of illiteracy, while others applaud it as having tremendous educational potential. Grants are sought and given, research institutes established, conferences and workshops held—endlessly, so it seems. And yet with all this activity, a persistent dissatisfaction remains for the basic problem—how to motivate the reluctant writer.

During the 1979–1980 academic year, the visual-narrative method of writing was implemented in two third-grade classes and one sixth-grade class at the Edith C. Baker Elementary School in the Brookline public school system. The three classroom teachers and I worked together to evaluate students in terms of both their verbal and their visual skills. It soon became clear that any given class could be divided into four basic types of students, each type representing approximately 25 percent of the class. They can be described as follows:

A. High visual and high verbal skills.
B. High visual and low verbal skills.
C. Low visual and high verbal skills.
D. Low visual and low verbal skills.

Type A students are most likely to be characterized as gifted, since they are the students who thrive on being challenged and seem equal to any task or assignment, whether verbal or visual. These students benefit from the visual-narrative method of writing and can obviously benefit from any approach that is challenging and creative.

Type B students are those who excel in all visual assignments but seem to have great difficulty with the normal academic tasks that are basically verbal. Because these students seem to resist the translation of visual insight and understanding into words, whether oral or written, they frequently do not progress well academically, do not test well with instruments of achievement that are almost exclusively verbal in nature, and are very likely to be frustrated because of peer and parental pressures with the consequent erosion of self-esteem. These are the students who benefit most from the visual-narrative method of writing and are most likely to show dramatic improvement.

Type C students are those who have very limited visual skills but significant and even superior verbal skills. Since academic progress is predicated very largely on analytic-verbal competencies, these students are likely to do very well in school and may ignore the visual arts as a "waste of time" on the notion that they neither need nor can benefit significantly from the visual-narrative method of writing.

Type D students are the unfortunate few who have little ability in either visual or verbal skills and are most likely the students having great difficulties in all subjects. Among such students all possible methods of instruction should be tried, including the visual-narrative method, since whatever works will be beneficial.

Using this typology, it was concluded that up to 75 percent of the students in any given class could show significant and even dramatic improvement in writing through the visual-narrative method of instruction.

Also, during the 1979–1980 school year at the Baker School, twenty-five students (or about one-third of the total enrollment of the three classes) were identified as having difficulties with the act of writing. Their difficulties ranged from "moderate" (students needing additional help) to "severe" (students either refusing, resisting, or unable to write at grade level). This classification provided valuable information for the design of lessons and projects tailored to the visual/verbal aptitudes of specific students. This information, in turn, enabled the teachers to use the visual-narrative approach when focusing on specific problems in writing.

Additional support for my observations can be found in the work of the noted British encephalographer, Dr. Grey Walter. In 1953, he estimated on the basis of brain-wave analysis that 15 percent of the population thinks in visual terms, 15 percent in verbal terms, and the rest in varying degrees of visual and verbal terms (Taylor, 1979, 214). I believe the 10 percent difference between my simple observation and his statistical study can be accounted for by comparing the terms *generally* in my observation and *exclusively* in Dr. Walter's study (refer again to Figure I–1). The 15-percent populations are represented by the black-and-white extremes of the value chart. My 25 percent would include some of the gray areas. Although I have not done a statistical study, I have found by simple observation that most classes of average size tend to divide rather equally into the four *general* groups that I have described, each being approximately 25 percent of any given class. Whatever the precise empirical statistic, it is plain to see that significant numbers of children are obviously ill served by most language-arts programs if it is the purpose of such programs to be responsive to individual aptitudes.

Since children are both visual and verbal learners, and since both images and words are effective and compatible tools for communication, it seems obvious that the two should never be separated. Unfortunately, the traditional understanding of the visual image has been far too narrow and greatly misunderstood by most language-arts teachers. Arnheim (1969) explains that "the arts are based on perception, and perception is disdained because it is not assumed to involve thought" (3). It follows that visual thinking, as a reality in and of itself, tends to be overlooked or misunderstood entirely. So often the visual is simply identified with television shows or computer terminals, with photographic reproductions, book illustrations, or films. All of these various phenomena are visual, to be sure, but in highly externalized and contrived ways that have virtually nothing to do with the visual thinking of the child. Arnheim (1969) points out that the mere presentation of visual material does not automatically guarantee its understanding. He asks, "How much do we know about what exactly children and other learners see when they look at a textbook illustration, a film, a television program?" (308–9). In short, the concern here is *not* with the visual creativity of teachers or the adult manufacturers of educational materials. The concern is rather with discovering *how the visual thinking natural to the child can be used to facilitate the development of improved writing skills.*

VERBAL LEARNERS AND LEARNING

Verbal learners are generally easier to identify. They are comfortable with words and respond very positively to verbal stimuli. They are not afraid to volunteer during class discussions, they willingly read their stories to the rest of the class, and they don't resist the prospect of reworking a given assignment in order to improve it. Because these students are at home in a "worded" world, they follow verbal directions easily and function satisfactorily in the predominantly verbal classrooms of our verbal schools and in the workplace of our highly verbal society. Chances are this type of student will be identified as being "bright," since the prevailing criteria brought to bear on intelligence testing and overall performance are so heavily weighted to verbal aptitudes—even the so-called visual parts! Many, if not most, educators take for granted that language ability is a very accurate overall indicator of intellectual ability. But Arnheim (1969) argues that verbal language is "overrated" and that the "visual medium is enormously superior . . . its principal virtue being its ability to represent shapes in both two-and three-dimensional space, compared to the one-dimensional sequence of verbal language" (232). Even though many things may be happening simultaneously, verbal language is limited to describing one thing at a time. And Gardner (1982) speaks to the uniqueness of the visual when he says that "an artistic medium provides the means for coming to grips with ideas and emotions of great significance, ones that cannot be articulated and mastered through ordinary conversational language" (90).

This might be why many artists are reluctant to "explain" their works to interested viewers—especially critics. They will resist this invitation by saying something like, "I'll let you decide," or agree to whatever is perceived by the critic as being the "essence" of the work of art. Artists, of course, are very pleased to have an appreciative following of influential "experts," and their frequently agreeable cordiality can be motivated by all sorts of reasons—not the least of which is economics. But underneath it all—at least for a great many artists— is the common conviction that what is being said in a particular painting or sculpture cannot be said through or reduced to a verbalization of its meaning. As Isadora Duncan once said, "If I could say it, I wouldn't have to dance it" (Gardner, 1982, 90).

Why then do most language-arts teachers take for granted that words are the primary and even the exclusive means of communication? Because speaking, listening, reading, and writing appear to be the most essential skills in the educative process, it is assumed that the only way teaching can take place is through words. Therefore, in the writing of stories, teachers use words to elicit more words from their students (Greene and Petty, 1975; Calkins, 1986). On the other hand, a visual approach to writing *translates* more effectively the untapped reservoir of visual experience and understanding into words, thereby improving the writing skills of the many children who are "reluctant writers" simply because they are visual learners.

Another way to describe the basically visual child would be to reflect on everyday classroom events. Most language-arts teachers have relatively high verbal competencies. Because this is the case, they are not particularly self-conscious about verbal demonstrations during the course of instruction. From time to time, however, a teacher must make a point by drawing a figure or a symbol on a chalkboard. But the classroom teacher is so often uncomfortable with this kind of instruction, he or she might preface the demonstration by saying, "Please forgive me—I'm not an artist, but it looks something like this . . ." If the art teacher were present, of course, he or she would be asked to make the visual point, just as the so-called class artists might be asked to extend their services, thereby "making use" of their talents!

If language-arts teachers can begin to recognize these visual-verbal inclinations and competencies in themselves, then they are on the road to being able to diagnose much more effectively the visual-verbal profile of their own students. Every teacher, of course, has a general awareness of this profile after just a few encounters with students. But too often this profile, if compiled from a rather superficial and one-sided verbal battery of information—such as permanent records, classroom participation, and classroom behavior—is completely inadequate. None of these provides a complete picture of any student, but the basically visual child loses out most.

Thus, it is my contention that the diagnostic piece that is missing can be more effectively "shown" than "explained." In order to demonstrate this point, study the four drawings in Figure 2–1 in order to become familiar with them. Next, match the correct drawing(s) with the following statements:

1. One of the drawings is by a student of exceptional intelligence, possibly genius IQ. _____
2. One of the drawings is by a mentally retarded student who is not in regular academic classes. _____

Figure 2–1

Images for the
visual quiz

3. Of the three students in regular academic settings, two are considered to have low ability in writing skills. _____ _____

4. The student with very high verbal abilities is regarded as a model student. _____

5. One of the students has become a discipline problem, probably out of frustration with conventional, highly verbal methods of instruction. _____

6. One of the students is regarded as the "class artist" and his academic teachers say, "Isn't it nice he can do something well!" _____

7. Two of the students are sixth-grade boys. _____ _____

8. Two of the students are seventh-grade boys. _____ _____

ANSWERS   1. A 2. D 3. B & C 4. A 5. B 6. C 7. A & C 8. B & D

If responses lead to surprise, don't regard them as curious or unimportant; view them against the following analyses. They are useful in assisting language-arts teachers to develop a sensitivity as well as a diagnostic tool that will enable them to assess the abilities of their students more accurately.

Drawing A exhibits what most artists would regard as very inadequate and undeveloped visual skills. The stick figure bears little similarity to the way the human form is seen, and the tree is a symbolic stereotype that any primary child could render. The placement of the swing suggests a basic understanding of perspective but nothing more. Nevertheless, what we see here is an ability to abstract for the sake of symbolic communication. But because this student is outstanding academically, neither the school community nor his family is particularly concerned that he has such limited visual skills. This limitation is not viewed as a handicap. His art teacher, on the other hand, evaluates him as visually "retarded."

Drawing B shows a very advanced understanding of the body, not only in its various parts, but also in the action and movement of the body. The side view is convincingly portrayed, and its proportion to the dragonlike beast heightens the drama of the drawing. This student, as mentioned above, "sees" very naturally but seems frustrated by conventional, verbal modes of instruction. This probably contributes to his discipline problem.

Drawing C manifests sound understanding of the body as well as the ability to depict a highly stressful situation, namely, being bitten on the leg by a very strange but convincingly real imaginary creature. The two bolts of lightning add to the drama of this situation.

Drawing D is primitive in some respects, such as the depiction of arms and fingers with sticklike lines. But aside from this, there is much more visual information than in Drawing A concerning the rest of the figures. The circular shapes and curved lines represent the movement of spacecrafts from the celestial to the terrestrial sphere. But it must be recalled that this student is quite severely mentally retarded, whereas the student who drew Drawing A is considered gifted!

Many classroom teachers are pleased to discover that students such as C and D "can do *something* well" since they are otherwise low in all academic respects. They are similarly frustrated with students like B who seem to have academic aptitude but will not apply themselves and cooperate. What these teachers fail to recognize is that a mode of cooperation and instruction *does* exist, and that is focusing on visual aptitude and proficiency. The problem is that many teachers do not know how to transfer this to academic subjects—especially writing. The visual child can be taught to improve his or her writing skills not *in spite of* visual inclinations, but *through* them. It is simply a matter of "translation" from the visual to the verbal mode, the "bridge" to which Ben Shahn refers as mentioned previously (Morse, 1972, 44).

Looking back to Drawing D, one might wonder how, in fact, it is known that the circular shapes and curved lines represent the movement of space vehicles. This representation would not be particularly obvious unless the teacher took the time to talk with the student. Again, we must place a great deal of importance on dialogue *with* students. In this particular case, the student was asked to talk about his drawing and to explain further anything that was not understood. Since this student has tremendous difficulties expressing himself verbally, he could easily become so self-conscious that he couldn't say anything at all, but when he was interpreting his own drawing, he seemed to forget about himself, and his verbal communication was relatively easy to understand. He was, in fact, "translating" his drawing.

It is very important to note repeatedly that visual children don't automatically translate from pictures to words. They need careful instruction and practice to make an effective translation from what they know visually to what they can say verbally. Visual children, like highly verbal children, simply assume that their favorite mode of expression is as clear to others as it is to themselves. Unassisted, they minimize the details of expression in the less-favored mode because they think it unimportant and not worth the effort. I contend that it is. Rudolf Arnheim seems to agree:

> Everything we are learning about the mental functioning of scientists and artists strengthens the conviction that the intimate interaction between intuitive and intellectual functioning accounts for the best results in both fields. And the same is true for the average schoolchild and student. (Mitchell, 1980, 179)

ONE INFORMS THE OTHER

When language-arts teachers become aware that children are both visual and verbal learners, and that both pictures and words tell stories, they can make better use of this information in order to educate the "total" child. Pictures can provide additional information to words for the visual learner, and words can provide additional information to pictures for the verbal learner. One informs the other. When children are educated with both the visual and the verbal modes of learning (the verbal mode being presupposed), they can move back and forth between these domains without effort. When the verbal mode is no longer able to provide information and insight, the child then moves naturally and comfortably to the visual mode for new insight and information. For example, a child may begin a story with words, and after writing a paragraph or two feel that he or she does not have enough detailed information to continue. At this point, the child should stop writing and draw a picture of the troublesome part of the story in order to gather more detailed information. When the student feels that this has been accomplished, then he or she can move back to the written form with more than enough data to augment and to continue what has already been written.

A page from a story by a third-grade boy demonstrates how easily one can move from the verbal to the visual mode and back again (see

Figure 2–2). This is a student with above-average ability with words as well as with pictures, and he feels comfortable using both to communicate his ideas. His classroom teacher values both modes of learning equally, demonstrating this in separate and integrated assignments, and encouraging proficiency in both. If it "pleased" his teacher to use only the verbal mode, the child would soon neglect the visual thinking as being inferior and of less value. By such an oversight, children can be systematically denied the potential of the visual.

Figure 2–2

Moving back and forth between the verbal and visual modes of expression

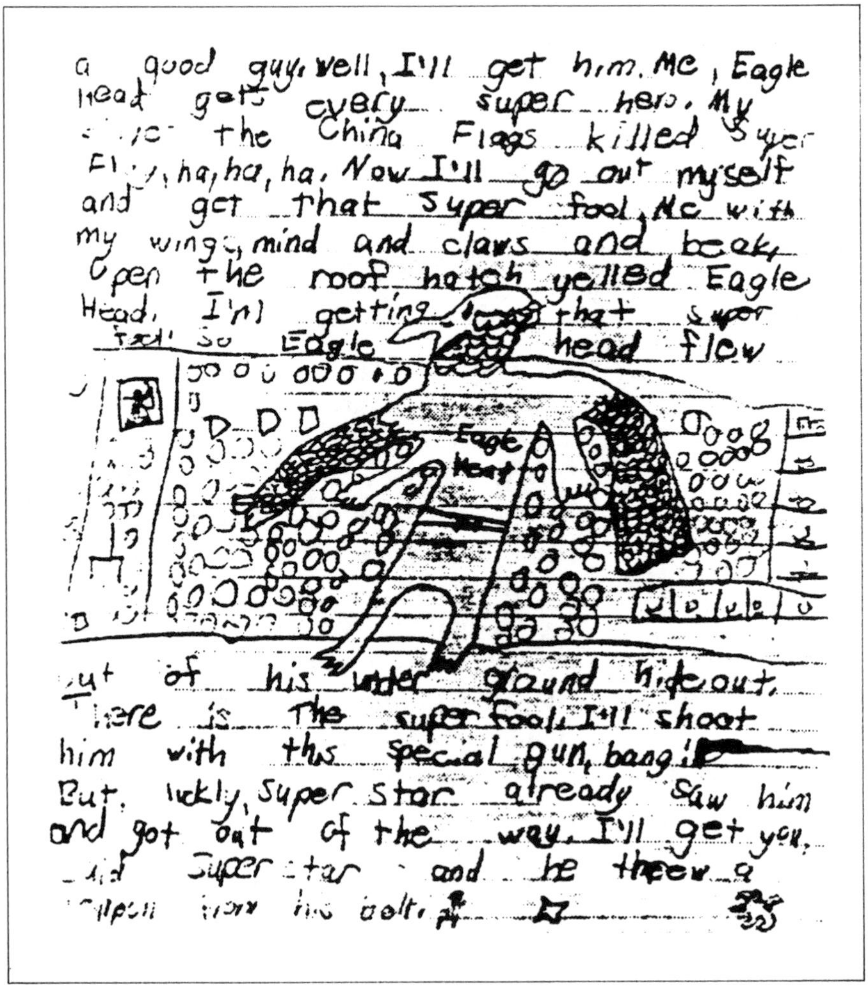

The language-arts teacher can accomplish this task very effectively, however. The teacher needn't be highly visual or an accomplished artist. Once this is understood, some teachers change their entire style of teaching as they grow to recognize the value and the need for visual communication even though they themselves once felt visually insecure. To be effective in using the visual-narrative method, one need not become an artist, but one must be aware and able to identify those children who could benefit most from this method. Indeed, it may be precisely because a given child is highly visual that verbal aptitudes seem underdeveloped or deficient. But once such children have been identified, the visual can be deployed in such a way as to enhance writing and verbal expression. Thus it is important to incorporate into writing programs such visual devices and techniques as will enable the visual learner to reach full verbal potential in order to compete in our highly verbal, "worded" world. It is precisely the incorporation of these visual techniques that constitutes the essence of this new approach to the teaching of writing. It is especially designed to serve the misunderstood children in our schools—the so-called problem readers and writers. It is not intended to displace existing methods of instruction, but to augment them.

As a case in point, I once attended a seventh-and eighth-grade faculty meeting during which "problem learners" were being discussed. Five students were presented as being in this category for various reasons: two students were identified as having learning difficulties and three as having behavior problems. I knew all five students as being highly visual. This was the common denominator in an otherwise conflicting diagnostic situation. But this situation cannot be confined to a particular example, for it happens again and again.

Visual communication is much too important to be neglected any longer. Artists, of course, have been aware of its importance for centuries. But artists have also been similarly identified as "strange" and "different" in comparison with so-called normal people. Nevertheless, what artists produce is regarded as "high culture"—the monuments of civilization and value. What this method recognizes, then, is the kind of thinking that underlies the production of great art on the notion that it has implications for communication and learning.

Before describing the application of this method, I will first demonstrate that it does, in fact, make a difference in the writing skills of students. Some of the changes are subtle, others more obvious and dramatic. *Please note that in each of the following examples, spelling and grammatical errors are left uncorrected*, whether they occurred in the development of characters, settings, or the plot of a story. Such initial efforts should be considered raw material for the student to work with under the guidance of the language-arts teacher. In each instance, the students were given as much time as necessary to complete the writing.

Characters   The following six examples of student writing demonstrate how the development of a character can change when the visual mode of learning is deployed as a complement to the verbal mode.

EXAMPLE 1:   A SIXTH-GRADE BOY

Before

The Big Guy
James weighs 240 pounds and use to be the champ. He beat Mohamad Ali for the crown. He's 38 know and he has drugs and pot. He's been in jail for 5 years and that ended his carrear. He's had a tough time finding a job. His face is scared. He wares a ripped T shirt with knee pants. He's trying to make a come back in the boxing world. He's black.

Visual-Narrative Drawing
See Figure 2–3 for the visual-narrative drawing of "The Big Guy."

After

The Big Guy
The lonely man stood in a ring holding tight to the ropes. His head was bald. His chest was hairy and sweaty. His legs looked like they were planted to the ground like stumps. His muscels were relaxed in the dark ring. His mouth looked mean and tough the way it was formed. He was solid looking. His boxing gloves had blood stains on them. His still body structure glowed in the darkness. He braced himself against the ropes. His white pants had red strips. The hair on his chin prickled out like thorns.

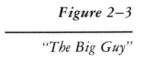

Figure 2–3

"The Big Guy"

Comment. This student has very highly developed visual skills. His language-arts teacher identified him as being very low in verbal skills. He has always had difficulty writing. His teacher was impressed with the quality of his writing when he used the visual-narrative approach. She is convinced that this is the best method to further develop his language skills.

EXAMPLE 2:   A SIXTH-GRADE BOY

Before

Harvey Haddix, Jr.
Old pitcher for the Pirates, Cardinals, Reds, and Orials. Coach for Pirates now. Brown hair. Wight 170. Height 5' 9". Born 1938. Lives in Pitsburg. In 1959 he pitched 12 perfect innings only to lose in the 13th. Looks like a fish. He is white.

Visual-Narrative Drawing

See Figure 2–4 for the visual-narrative drawing of "Harvey Haddix, Jr."

Figure 2–4

"Harvey Haddix,
Jr."

After

Harvey Haddix was pitching on the pitching mound. He wore blue sweat soxs. The left sneaker was a blue nike. The right one was a red Adidas sneaker. This year he was a rookie all star. He liked to pitch in baseball. His pants were white but had dirt stains. His shirt had the great name Pirates. He had blue shoelaces to match his soxs. His legs, thighs, shoulders, hands and his whole body ached. His glove was a Wilson. The ball he pitched was high quality leather. Sweat drops wet his hair. The Pirates fans were sad, low and angry. The Braves fans were happy. Two Braves fans made fun of him from the box seats. He saw evil foreign eyes look at him. The webbing of his glove was falling apart. He lost the game. This game was a memorable event in history as he walked of the field a star lit up his number "13."

Comment. This boy is considered to have above-average visual and verbal skills. While the second piece of writing is not finished (as in the case of the previous example), all the raw material is there for close editing in order to produce the final draft of which the student can be justifiably proud.

EXAMPLE 3:   A SIXTH-GRADE BOY

Before

Dog

My dog has brown eyes, golden fur, is very smart, likes to catch fish, is very handsome, he is a good watch dog, he is as fast as a leopart and eats anything. He is called a Golden Retrever. His name is Scooter.

Visual-Narrative Drawing

See Figure 2–5 for this boy's visual-narrative drawing.

After

My Dog

My dog gets very hungry wile running. He likes to sit under trees. He loves walking through the leaves. He sometimes stars at the blue sky with the white clouds. He likes eating the green grass. He also keeps me warm. If you hurt him he will be mean. He has big ears. He also has brown eyes and sharp teeth. His tail is very short. His fur is golden. His fur is very long. He has

Figure 2–5

"My Dog"

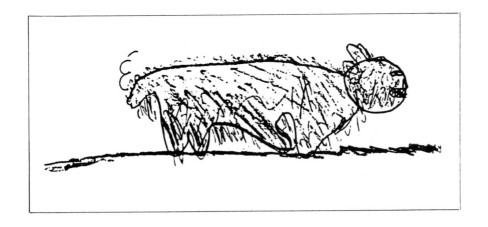

long legs. He also has a wet nose. He hates looking at the sun's
rays. He gets very itchy if small ants get into his fur. He hates
stepping on hot sand. He loves swimming in the cold water. His
feet are very rough. His head is smooth. He also likes catching
fish. His head is also soft. He is very big. Also he is very furry.
When he is very happy at someone he wiggles his tail. He
doesn't weigh very much.

Comment. This student was identified as being very weak in both
verbal and visual skills. Nevertheless, the visual-narrative approach to
writing was highly successful since it provided him with a means of
developing much more detailed information about his character. In
sum, the student does not have to be a "good artist" for this method
to work very effectively.

EXAMPLE 4:   A SIXTH-GRADE BOY

Before

Dinosour
My dinosour is smart, kind, handsome, and very tall. My
dinosaur is a Taranasaurs Rex He's 50 feet tall and weighs 3,000
pounds. He's very strong but jentle.

Visual-Narrative Drawing
Figure 2–6 shows this boy's visual-narrative drawing.

After

Dinosaur
My Dinosaur is very big. He's the king of all Dinosaurs. He's
breathing heavely but he's vicious looking when he's angry.
When he's walking he walks like a cowboy. He's superier in our
land because he's tall and he's muscular so he could easily crush
us though he's very gentle. He could breathe fire with
tremendous force. He has evel looking eyes which he uses to find
food. He's skaly and cours. The skales look like waves, waves
small and large. He weighs alot about 3,000 pounds. His snout
is round and his teeth are sharp. He has a smooth head which
doesn't have any skales. His hands always seem to be grasping.

Figure 2–6

"Dinosaur"

He likes stepping over a tree once in a while. We have a volcano which always starts errupting once in a while too. The smkey lave starts oozing down the rocky and rough side. You would be able to find him in the forest because he's large and plump but we don't make fun of him. Otherwise we live a heathy life.

Comment. This student has high visual skills and very low verbal skills. His language-arts teacher was astonished to discover that he was capable of developing a sustained, narrative description of a character. There are also interesting psychological dimensions to this piece. The student himself is small and rather frail, but is part of a family of athletes who value physical strength and achievement. Since this student's artistic ability is not valued by his family, it served only as an escape. But in this case it greatly facilitated his language skills. This is a good illustration for an effective utilization of both verbal and visual modes of instruction in language-arts curricula.

EXAMPLE 5:   A SIXTH-GRADE BOY

Before

The Mean Old Man

The mean old man wore a hat and a long coat. His lip was crooked and he had only 3 front teeth. He had a bad spot on the top of his head and some white strands at the side. His eyes were slanted and he had bags under his eyes. His nose was smooshed in. He had a scar on his left cheek. He smoked too.

He was leaning against a pole at the end of the street, waiting for his car.

It was a gloomy, foggy day, it had just rained. The sun was hidden by forty clouds it seemed like.

Visual-Narrative Drawing

See Figure 2–7 for the visual-narrative drawing of "This Mean Old Man."

Figure 2–7

―――――――――

"The Mean Old Man"

After

The Mean Old Man

The mean old man leaned on a post on 22 Avenue. He put his bloody hand in his lapeled coat. He started to wonder if the car was going to come. He then took a KOOL cigaret and started to smoke. He wore a rugged hat on top of his bald spot, little white strands sprung out. He had a scar soaring down his left cheek, right down to his crooked mouth and on to his slanted eyes, while passing his smooshed nose. Water started to build up on his feet. His double chin reached his mouth and looked like a slash. Then the cigaret slipped threw his mouth because his 3 front teeth were missing. Bags occured under his crooked eyes. Mist started pouring over the mean old man and his cloths. Then the black cadilac pulled up. The man waved a motion to the mean old man to hop in. The car dissapered in the mist.

Comment. This student has very high visual skills and a great deal of difficulty including detail in his writing. He was asked to imagine a character that might become part of a story later in his work. The first writing included everything he could think of about the character. The second writing is about the same character but was preceded by a drawing of the character.

EXAMPLE 6: POEM BY A THIRD-GRADE GIRL

Before

Scissor
Razor sharp,
Cuts through paper as if it
was rolling down a hill,
Swiftly it finishes the paper,
and the paper is in half.

Visual-Narrative Drawing
See Figure 2–8 for this girl's visual-narrative drawing.

After

Figure 2–8

"*My Scissor*"

My Scissor
The crocidile,
eats it's paper, It's fangs bite,
Like a werewolf.
It's sharp claws chop through the paper.
CUT! CUT! CHOP! CHOP!
As the swords and knifes come together.
The stork opens it's beak
And then smashes it closed,
The alligator snaps for its food.
That's my Scissor.

Comment. This student has very good verbal skills but is considered average visually. This is a good example of how visual expression can even be helpful when students' verbal skills are better than their visual skills. In this case, the student wrote a good first poem. Then the visual mode inspired her to write a much better poem, experimenting with far more imaginative language.

Settings If characters are placed into a well-described setting, the story becomes much more interesting. The following three examples of student writing demonstrate how the description of a setting can be enhanced through the visual-narrative method of writing.

THE LANGUAGE-ARTS PROGRAM

63

EXAMPLE 1: A SIXTH-GRADE BOY

Before

It was a dark, stormy night. Detective Harper and I couldn't sleep so we . . .

Visual-Narrative Drawing

Figure 2–9 shows this boy's visual-narrative drawing.

After

It was a stormy, Autumn night, a night on which you think something would happen. The large oak tree in the front lawn cast sinister shadows upon the house. The rain hitting the roof sounded like rain hitting a roof. A sudden bolt of lightning shook the house. A distant wolf atop a hill overlooking the moors of England let out a loud howl. Detective Harper and I couldn't sleep so we . . .

Figure 2–9

"It was a dark, stormy night"

Comment. This was the beginning of a mystery story. The language-arts teacher wanted the opening setting to establish a specific mood appropriate to the rest of the story. This student has about

average visual and verbal skills. But before the application of the visual-narrative mode, he could not think of any way to expand his opening sentence. This is a good example of what could be termed "facilitating the transaction and translation" between the visual and the verbal. But it is something that verbal criticism alone cannot accomplish, for verbal critique usually consists of the teacher imposing ideas upon the student. What we have in all these instances are examples of spontaneous enhancements coming from the students themselves.

EXAMPLE 2:   A SIXTH-GRADE GIRL

Before

California Boardwalk
This place is a fun place. People roller skating down the board people riding bicycles. Palm trees standing bring shade the ocean roaring against the rocks. People renting skates men and women under plam trees talking. It is nice and worm with a brisk wind.

Visual-Narrative Drawing

See Figure 2–10 for this girl's "California Boardwalk" visual-narrative drawing.

Figure 2–10

"California Boardwalk"

After

California Boardwalk *(poetic form)*
People walking down the boardwalk
Riding bicycles
Roller skating
Having fun
Children swimming in the ocean
Sailboats swiftly sailing by
People admiring the dark misty blue ocean
Palm trees standing while the wind swishes the leaves
People eating ice cream while it drips from their chin
Food stand waiting for customers
The white caps bumping against the rocks
The foam dissolving quickly
Musicians playing waiting for some nice person to hand
out money
The monkey collecting the money they do get
Sea Guls giving the call and their mates come a
running
Warm beautiful sunny windy on this California
Boardwalk.

Comment. This student was asked to describe a place. Before starting the second draft, she asked if it could be in the form of a poem. She obviously benefited from a visually facilitated shift from prose to poetry.

EXAMPLE 3:   A SIXTH-GRADE BOY

Before

This was the first time I had gone to a fishing resort. We got our little cabin, a motor boat and at the main house we were served all three meals each day.

Visual-Narrative Drawing

Figure 2–11 shows this boy's visual-narrative drawing.

Figure 2–11

"This was the first time I had gone to a fishing resort"

After

This was the first time I had gone to a fishing resort. When I got to the cabin I saw the lake, the dock, and the birch trees, and then the old oak tree. This tree looked like it was about to break any second. It was a tall grayish brown tree. It was rough and wide. It's roots were coming out of the ground in all places. When the wind blew you could hear this old, towering tree creek.

There was an island in the middle of the lake. The ground next to the dock had split off and crumbled into the water. I could hardly wait to go. We got out little cabin, a motor boat, and at the main house we were served all three meals each day.

Comment. This boy's language-arts teacher became very frustrated with him because, as he put it, "All he wants to do is draw!" By comparing the "before" and the "after" writing, it is obvious that this student's artistic inclination should be put to use helping to improve the writing skills he otherwise resists.

Plots Teachers often mention that some children have great difficulty sequencing the plot of a story into logical order. The visual-narrative approach is particularly useful in this area. The following two examples of student writing illustrate this clearly.

EXAMPLE 1: A THIRD-GRADE BOY

Before

The Ghost of Zimbabwe

"Build those walls!" said the Mambo. "Hi, I'm the ghost of Zimbabwe." I've roamed these Savannas for 300 years." This valley is called the home of the dead! "When a mambo is a chief dies he is buried. "Roswe plays Songs". If it is an important person they build walls around him. The Rozwe had a sekret.

The
n
d

Figure 2–12

"The Ghost of Zimbabwe"

Visual-Narrative Drawing

See Figure 2–12 for this boy's visual-narrative drawing.

After

The Ghost of Zimbabwe

Once many years ago Mambo yelled at the Rozwi to build walls
and to haul granite. It was a sunny day near the temple. Some
Rozwi were mad. Kun and Tonto were the maddest. They hated
to haul granite and build walls and trenches. Before they worked
together in the valley they were enemies. Now they are best
friends. That night Kun and Tonto had a meeting. They were
going to kill mambo. Just then a messenger came by and heard
them talking about the mambo and ran as fast as he could to the
mambo. When he got there he told the mambo. When the
mambo heard this he called his guards. That night Kun and
Tonto killed the mambo and fled.

The

n

d

Comment. The first piece of writing is simply a list of facts gathered
during a recently completed social studies unit even though the assignment was to compose a story. There is no sense of any logical sequence
of events and only a very fragmentary narrative quality. The second
piece of writing, however, shows great improvement in both respects.
Drawing helped the student to visualize the order of events.

EXAMPLE 2:   A THIRD-GRADE BOY

Comment. This student was becoming very frustrated because he
was to write a story about a character he had drawn a picture of, but
he just couldn't think of anything to write. This is not an uncommon
situation for many students. He had drawn a picture of a rabbit with
a carrot growing in the ground beside him. He glued white cotton on
top of the rabbit drawing in order to make him appear three-dimensional. He began his story with "Once upon a time . . ." but couldn't
get any further. We talked for a while about his favorite comic strips
and how pictures can tell stories. He was given some storyboard paper
(paper with boxes printed on it), but paper simply folded into sections
can also be used. He immediately got an idea for the beginning of a

visual story. After this, all the teacher had to do was ask questions such as:

- What will happen next?
- What is the weather like?
- Is he happy or sad?
- Why does he look this way?

As he drew (see Figure 2–13), it was observed that he changed expressions on the little boy's face from happy to disappointed to sad. He verbalized the story as he went along. He worked out a logical change of sequence in the weather. For example, he said that it wouldn't rain on the day the little boy was watering the carrot seeds!

Written Story

Eran and Flufy

Once there was a boy named Eran who loved carrots.

So he went to a shop and he bought a carrot seed. It was $ .10.

He went home and he planted it. The next day he watered it. After school Eran was happy because it was growing. In the morning it was raining but he was even happyer becease in two days there would be a carrot for me! Fiv days past and in a bay it be ripe. One bay to go a miracle had hapened. A rainbow appeared.

Later that day he went to the place where the carrot was. But he did see a rabbit with his carrot the boy started to cry. The rabbit opligied [apologized] to Eran. The boy agread. So the rabbit and Eran went to the park and Eran asked you want to be my pet.

He said yes Eran asked you wand a name the rabbit said yes so they called him Flufy.

The

Eend

BENEFITS OF VISUAL-NARRATIVE DRAWING FOR STUDENTS AND TEACHERS

When the third-grade student finished the sequence of eleven drawings necessary to tell his story about "Eran and Fluffy," he was ready to

write it with words and to do so with minimum effort or frustration. When he finished writing, he said the following:

> I feel good. It's the longest story I've ever written. The pictures helped a lot. They helped me to remember the story. Planning a picture story was easier because drawing is easier for me. It takes a long time to learn how to write, but I've been drawing as long as I can remember.

These remarks are typical of most students who are effectively helped by this method:

- Drawing helped me because then I could look at it and say what I thought.
- Drawing helped me because it gave me ideas.
- Drawing helped because it gave me more description in my story.
- Drawing my character helped me to understand it much better.
- Drawing helped me to remember details.
- Drawing helped because it was more fun and I could see what was really happening in my story.
- Sometimes I have the answer in my head, but I don't know how to say it. When I can see it, I can say it.
- I think drawing is helpful because you can see what you are thinking and that way it would be easier to write it down. For example, when I was writing my first draft of my adventure, it was confusing because I could only picture it in my head. But when I started to draw, it was less confusing and much easier to write.

The following is a conversation I had with a third-grade student who had been using the visual-narrative method of writing:

TEACHER: Do you think writing and drawing help each other?
STUDENT: Yes, definitely.
TEACHER: In what way?
STUDENT: I can see what I want to write about and it becomes clearer.
TEACHER: What becomes clearer?
STUDENT: What I want to say.
TEACHER: Couldn't you write this without drawing?
STUDENT: Well, it would be a lot shorter and there wouldn't be as

many descriptive words, such as "the bird flew fast" or "the bird is brown." The drawing gives me ideas.

TEACHER: Couldn't you just have a picture in your mind and then write?

STUDENT: No, because it would get fuzzy once in a while.

TEACHER: What do you mean?

STUDENT: Well, when someone talked to me the picture would disappear, or if someone came into the room or if there was a loud noise, I would lose the picture in my mind and I'd probably forget what I was going to say. But when the picture is right in front of me, I don't forget, and what I'm going to say comes right back again.

Teachers also benefit from including the visual-narrative method of instruction into their existing language-arts programs. As mentioned previously, two third-grade language-arts teachers and one sixth-grade language-arts teacher volunteered for this project because they wished to understand the visual element better and incorporate it into their own curriculum. Their curiosity had been stimulated by seeing that there were compatible elements in both curricula—for example, in the development of character, setting, and plot. Although they felt insecure with art activities and particularly with drawing, by working closely with them I was able to give them the support and confidence they needed to proceed.

Each teacher experimented by integrating the visual and verbal components in a variety of instructional settings. They worked with individual students and small groups, and they also developed lessons for the entire class. I was always available to them for consultation, and I also observed and assisted in their classrooms. After working with the project for the better part of an academic year, the three classroom teachers reflected on the insights they gained:

Creative writing is a very important part of our Language Arts program, and it must be pursued with great love and integrity. Often a child may ask or be asked to illustrate a story that he or she has completed writing. Occasionally a drawing or photograph provides the springboard for an original story. Sharing our stories aloud is always enjoyed by authors and listeners alike. Until now, however, I was seldom comfortable with having a student initiate a story through pictures. That would be spending a great deal of time and thought on something I thought less important than writing. Consequently, I never encouraged students to write and draw simultaneously, going back and forth naturally from one expression to the other. Now I realize that weaving words and pictures together may create a rich tapestry, and that this method is a new and rich area of collaboration in language arts. (F. Meller, personal communication, May 1980)

The students began to make real connections between their words and their pictures through this method. Until now I had been telling them that their words should create pictures in the reader's mind forgetting that these pictures must first be in the writer's mind. Through this approach students are able to adopt workable strategies for themselves and for their future writing. . . . Indeed, through this method the teacher is able to discover many important things about the student's writing style and personality. (C. Bencal, personal communication, May 1980)

The visual narrative approach to writing enables students to actually see a beginning, middle, and an end to their stories. When this happens, the child can write a fairly long story comfortably. Every child improved. . . . They learned how to improve verbal skills through visual narrative and how to move most effectively from one to the other. (M. Prager, personal communication, May 1980)

LANGUAGE-ARTS TEACHERS DON'T HAVE TO BE "GOOD ARTISTS"

Many classroom teachers become nervous at the very mention of the word *draw*. They may respond by saying, "I can't even draw a straight line," or "My art teacher laughed at my work when I was in fourth grade," or "I can draw stick figures, but that's about it!" This insecurity contributes to the extensive use of patterns, stencils, and prepackaged materials in the general elementary-school classroom. Since very few states require teacher candidates to take an art or an art-education course as part of their preparation for certification, it's not surprising that most elementary teachers lack confidence in this area. But even if they did take such a course, much of the problem would still remain because, as mentioned earlier, art educators have been primarily concerned with the "child artist" and not with the "child learner." This being the case, the mere taking of an art or art education course would not greatly contribute to the classroom teachers' understanding of the relationship between drawing and writing or help them to feel a sense of security in their ability to initiate or integrate drawing tasks in their classes.

Nevertheless, such a requirement would certainly help to alleviate some of the insecurities and misunderstandings of teachers if attention were paid to the "child learner." Certainly students—and above all, the visual learner—would reap great benefits from this kind of teacher preparation. Teachers do not need to be "good artists" in order to recognize and encourage the visual skills of their students. They simply need to be sensitive to their special abilities, knowledgeable as to how these abilities can be encouraged, and understand how these abilities can be used as a tool for learning in other areas of the curriculum, especially in the area of writing and the language arts.

Thus it is not a matter of teachers' going back to school to learn how to make art. The teachers' task is to learn how to recognize and identify the visual competencies of their students instead of simply overlooking them; they then need to actively encourage, facilitate, and integrate the visual and the verbal modes of expression and meaning into all areas of the writing curriculum. Only in this way will the potential of all students be better realized.

EVALUATING STUDENTS: WHAT TO LOOK FOR

Teachers should begin by observing the visual and verbal patterns of behavior of their students. They should also keep a careful and accurate record of these observations. It is best to do this immediately with a new class before one becomes too resigned to the "way" a certain class is. Traditionally teachers first notice the children who are eager to answer questions and the children who misbehave. It is usually assumed that the quiet ones are either too timid to talk, have nothing to say, or are too slow or dull to know the answer; they are therefore overlooked and/or misunderstood. However, "unless extended verbal information is highly stimulating," John Dixon (1983) explains, the minds of spatial children "have a tendency to wander off into an inner daydream world of personal images" and that, in fact, "this is often the child's preferred mode of cognition" (208).

Of course, the identification of visual learners is not as simple as this. Such identification, to the extent that it is necessary and requires categorization, must be based on far more comprehensive criteria. Teachers must first consider the reasons for timidity—especially insecurity with the use of words. It may be that a given child feels as inadequate verbally as the teacher feels inadequate visually! A child may be timid or afraid because he or she cannot articulate as well as others in the class. Dixon (1983) further explains:

> Unlike many other children, [spatial children] have little motivation to pursue language study for its own sake. Being inclined to take in the full sensory depth and breadth of the world around them, the very idea of spending hours scanning with one's eyes along rows of small black shapes called letters is antithetical to what life is about for these children. (197)

It is easy to ignore such children on the notion that they simply aren't interested. But this kind of resignation simply contributes to the child's lack of self-esteem. A far more constructive response is to attend to them more carefully by identifying the visual skills that more comfortably facilitate expression and meaning, and to encourage their use as a bridge to eventually serve the verbal mode.

Disruptive children may also be visual. This may not, at first, seem to be the case, since disruptive children may be erroneously identified as "verbal" simply because they are usually noisy and talking all the time. But one should not be fooled by this behavior. It's quite possible that the noisy, boisterous child developed these patterns of behavior out of frustration in reaction to acceptable verbal modes of expression. In other words, the child may be engaging in loud and disruptive behaviors in order to compensate for feelings of inadequacy at not being able to measure up to the standards of verbal expectations. Dixon (1983) suggests that this type of child "may reach the level of outright hostility toward others and exhibit aggressive behavior" (193). Children know from a very early age that it is verbal proficiency that really counts in school!

Collecting concrete information with respect to skills in visual communication can be done in a variety of ways. In any event, good record keeping is absolutely essential since these records will become the empirical basis for preparing lessons, parent conferences, remedial work, and conferences with other teachers and support staff, such as counselors and specialists.

Classroom teachers usually feel quite confident when they classify and rate the verbal skills of their students. After just a few writing lessons and oral activities, teachers begin to classify and/or group students as high, medium, or low in written and oral proficiency. Classes are frequently organized either formally or informally into groups based on this performance with continued assessment and evaluation informed by the fact that children learn at different rates of speed (Greene and Petty, 1975).

Visual-narrative skills can be measured in a similar way since the procurement of this data is essential to the progress of the visual child. The teacher may feel uncertain as to how to do this and lack confidence in judgment. The following lessons are offered as *one* way to begin evaluating the visual-narrative skills of students. They are intended to help language-arts teachers become familiar with the kinds of visual information they should look for in children's drawings. When teachers become more informed and more confident in their ability to identify visual-narrative skills, they should then be encouraged to develop their own, less formal evaluative procedures. The process that I am suggesting is intended only to be a beginning, a learning strategy for the language-arts teacher, not necessarily for the child.

EVALUATION STRATEGIES

By observing and studying the narrative drawing skills of students in grades one through eight over a period of several years, I determined that their drawings could be rank-ordered high, medium, and low on the basis of identifying the specific visual clues necessary to communicate an idea. The following evaluation lessons are provided to show how this process can take place.

Evaluation   Begin with a drawing lesson that emphasizes facial expressions. A
Lesson 1   short discussion about the many different human emotions is helpful in

getting children to think about differences in expression. The teacher should not mention "how" to draw these faces because the purpose is not to teach them how to draw. The purpose is rather to determine the degree to which students are naturally observant and who has a highly developed visual language.

The class should be instructed to fold a 9 × 12 piece of drawing paper into four parts, and then consecutively number the spaces 1, 2, 3, and 4 together with the words *happy, sad, angry*, and *surprised* or *frightened* (see Figure 2–14). After this has been done, the students should draw the same face, changing the expression to fit the word, in each square. Students should put their name on the reverse side of the paper.

This short drawing exercise provides a concrete piece of information upon which to base some evaluation. Keep in mind, however, that a final judgment of verbal skills would not be made on a single written exercise. The same should be true when evaluating visual expression. This first exercise is just a beginning, but a very important beginning. The evaluation should proceed through the following steps:

Figure 2–14

Diagram for facial-expression lesson

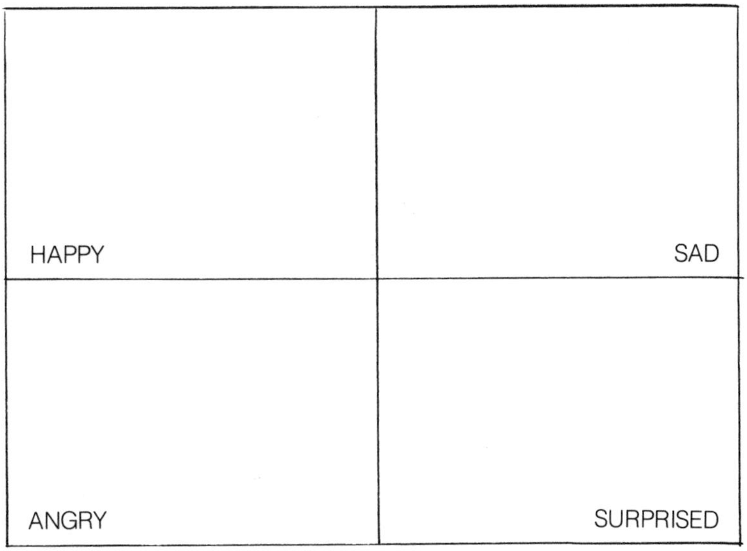

1. Go through the entire collection of drawings in order to become familiar with the total range of work. It is not necessary to check

HAPPY	SAD
ANGRY	SURPRISED

the name of the student at this point; in fact, it is better to avoid identification in order to be completely impartial.

2. Look through the collection again, but this time try to avoid being impressed by a well-stylized drawing and focus rather on the facial expressions. Pay special attention to the eyes (including the eyebrows), the mouth, and the lines of the face in the forehead and cheek areas.

3. Go through the collection a third time. This time make a preliminary judgment as to the degree of communication and/or expression by placing them into three piles labeled high, medium, and low. Place into "high" those drawings that change three or more features of the face to convey changes in expression. Place into "medium" those drawings that change two features and into "low" those drawings that change only one feature of the face to convey a given emotion. Some children will change only the mouth or the eyes (see Figure 2–15).

4. Look through the drawings again and make any changes necessary upon reconsideration. In some cases it might be necessary to have a + or − pile, but at this point it is a very general evaluation in a process that is going to become more precise as more information is gathered and evaluated.

5. Check the names of the students. Any surprises?

6. Record the evaluations using a personal system, making sure that the essential information of high, medium, or low is noted. Gradually, a sensitivity to the narrative dimension of a drawing will develop, along with new and valuable knowledge and understanding concerning the abilities of each student.

Evaluation Lesson 2

This sequence of drawings can be done very slowly, one part at a time for younger children or in one concentrated lesson for older students. The timing should be modified according to the grade level being taught.

Use the following Swiss folktale about a little elflike creature called *Erdluitle* (or Erdy for short) and proceed through the following steps:

1. Read the folktale to the entire class. Before reading, explain that an Erdluitle is a little, elflike fantasy creature.

HIGH

Figure 2–15

High, medium, and low facial expression

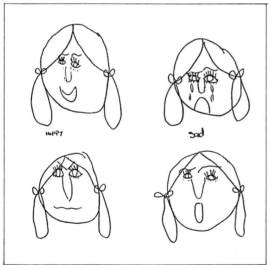

MEDIUM

LOW

It was common knowledge that the richest man in town was an incorrigible miser, but a poor sick relative decided nonetheless to ask him for help. The woman was so weak that she couldn't manage to walk herself and had to send her daughter. Neither the beauty, nor the youth, nor the obvious poverty of the girl made any impression on the scoundrel. He threw her out of his house in the middle of a terrible storm. Tired from the long walk and from lack of food, she started to cry. A young man saw her and took pity on her. He had only one cheese left but gave it to her without hesitation. "Take this, you need it more than I do," he said with a reassuring smile.

Even his kindness didn't change the girl's luck. She had only gone a few steps when the cheese slipped from her hands and rolled into a ravine.

"Now I have nothing to bring to my mother." She started to cry again.

Just then, a voice beside her said, "I found your cheese at the bottom of the ravine and have brought it back to you. I've also brought some tea for your mother. Give her some as soon as you get home, and she will recover."

The girl thanked the *Herdmanndli* (Erdluitle) profusely and hurried home before she had time to lose the second gift.

The herb tea quickly restored her mother's health and the cheese turned into pure gold. That night a storm loosened an avalanche, burying the miser's house. The girl and her mother lived in peace and comfort on the money from the golden cheese. (Arrowsmith, 1977, 45–46)

2. As the story is read, define any words the students may not understand, such as *miser, ravine*, and *scoundrel*. Some will also want more information about Erdluitles. Arrowsmith (1977) provides a great deal of additional information about these strange little creatures. For example, they are extremely reluctant to show their feet to animals, either because they are shy or because they do not want to reveal the source of their power. She says that Erdluitles are older than human beings and have more knowledge of the secret powers of nature. They can cause storms, floods, and avalanches,

and they know the secret of turning cheese and green leaves into gold and diamonds. Erdluitles are about one and one-half to three feet tall, their clothes are so long their goose or duck feet won't show, and some of them have animal ears. Their favorite foods are roots, berries, and peas. Erdluitles live in Switzerland and northern Italy, under rocks or underground in dark caves. Students seem to enjoy the humorous characterizations of Erdluitles, which definitely spark their fantastic imaginations.

3. Instruct the class to fold three pieces of 9″ × 12″ drawing paper into four parts, and number each part from 1 to 12 (as in Figure 2–14), only continue numbering consecutively throughout the three sheets of paper.

4. The next step consists of dividing the story into twelve distinctive parts, each demanding very specific visual information. This information can be provided by oral dictation or by listing the twelve parts on a handout sheet so that students can proceed at their own speeds. If oral dictation is used, it is necessary to repeat the verbal description several times so that students hear and consider each and every word. In the case of younger children, they might draw only one or two pictures per day. Only pencils should be used so that the thinking of each child will be recorded as directly as possible. Students should be told that *each* word in the story is important. Allow students enough time to complete each illustration to their own satisfaction. If time is limited, it would be impossible to learn the full extent of their visual thinking capabilities. Students should also be encouraged to go back and add more details at the end of the exercise.

List of Illustrations (12)

a. Title. The student can invent one and present it in box 1.
b. The mean old miser.
c. The sick, weak woman and her young beautiful daughter.
d. The old miser throwing the young girl out of his house in the middle of a terrible storm.
e. The young girl, tired and hungry, sits down and cries.
f. The young, smiling man offers her his last piece of cheese.
g. The young girl slips and the cheese falls into the ravine.
h. As she cries again, an Erdluitle appears next to her, explaining

that he retrieved the cheese from the ravine and also that he has tea for her mother.

  i. After the girl returns home, the tea restores her mother's health and the cheese turns into pure gold.

  j. That night, a storm causes an avalanche that buries the miser's house.

  k. The mother and daughter live in peace and comfort on the money from the golden cheese.

  l. The End.

5. The work is now ready for evaluation. After the teacher completes the evaluation process, an accurate measurement of the visual-narrative abilities of the entire class will be achieved. Additional observations will, of course, always be added to the record as they become available. The *Erdluitle* folktale will provide eleven additional entries to the record, with each illustration evaluated separately except for 1 and 12 (title and end), which are viewed as a single unit owing to their similarity. In the following account, elements of the illustration that should be examined carefully will be pointed out. Using this information, a three-step process of rating, similar to that used in the previous lesson on facial expressions, should be applied.

DRAWINGS 1 AND 12 Both of these drawings pertain primarily to the arrangement of words. Are the words presented in an interesting way? Are they decorated in any way? Are they made to look as though they have thickness ⊨ or three-dimensionality ⓔ ? Are the letters centered, balanced with an image, or arranged in the space in a careful way even if they are made with a single line ⊨ ? Does it seem as though there was little attention given to how the words or letters look? How many of these possibilities has the child included—three, two, one? Evaluate the work and place each into one of three groups (high, medium, low) and record the results (see Figures 2–16 and 2–17).

DRAWING 2 Was the student able to make this character look mean? Was the student able to make him look old? Was the student able to portray him as a miser? Did the child show three, two, or one of these characteristics? Separate the drawings into three groups and record the results (see Figure 2–18).

Figure 2–16

Drawing 1 for Erdluitle story: high, medium, and low ratings

HIGH

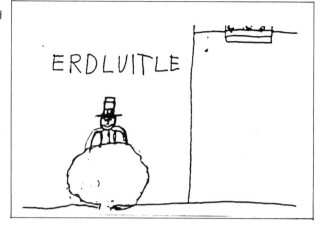

MEDIUM

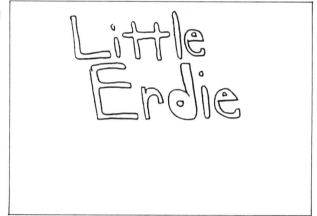

LOW

HIGH

Figure 2–17

Drawing 12 for Erdluitle story: high, medium, and low ratings

MEDIUM

LOW

HIGH

Figure 2–18

Drawing 2 for Erdluitle story: high, medium, and low ratings

MEDIUM

LOW

Figure 2–19

Drawing 3 for
Erdluitle story: high,
medium, and low
ratings

MEDIUM

LOW

DRAWING 3   Does the woman look sick and weak? Does the girl look young and
beautiful? Is there an obvious age difference between the two characters? Separate the drawings into three groups and record the results
(see Figure 2–19).

Figure 2–20

Drawing 4 for Erdluitle story: high, medium, and low ratings

HIGH

MEDIUM

LOW

DRAWING 4   Does the miser actually look as though he is throwing the girl? Does the student include at least part of the house, such as the door, to convey the information? Did the student show the storm? Separate and record (see Figure 2–20).

Figure 2-21

Drawing 5 for
Erdluitle story: high,
medium, and low
ratings

HIGH

MEDIUM

LOW

DRAWING 5   Does the student make the girl look tired and hungry? Is the student
able to make the character look as though she is sitting down? Is the
character crying? Divide and record (see Figure 2-21).

88

Figure 2–22

Drawing 6 for Erdluitle story: high, medium, and low ratings

HIGH

MEDIUM

LOW

DRAWING 6   Does the man look young? Is he smiling? Is he offering the cheese to the girl? Divide and record (see Figure 2–22).

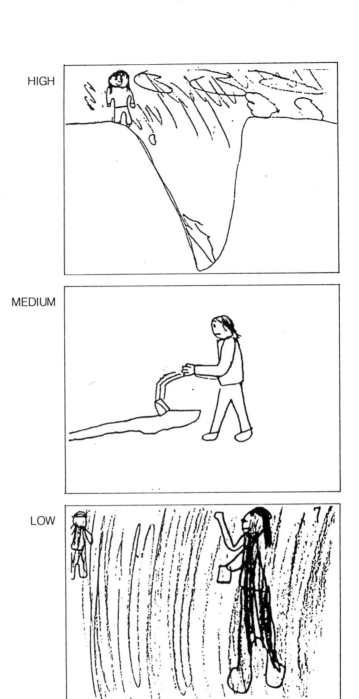

Figure 2–23

*Drawing 7 for
Erdluitle story: high,
medium, and low
ratings*

MEDIUM

LOW

DRAWING 7   Is the student able to show the character slipping? Does the student
show the cheese? A ravine? Divide and record (see Figure 2–23).

Figure 2–24

Drawing 8 for
*Erdluitle story: high,
medium, and low
ratings*

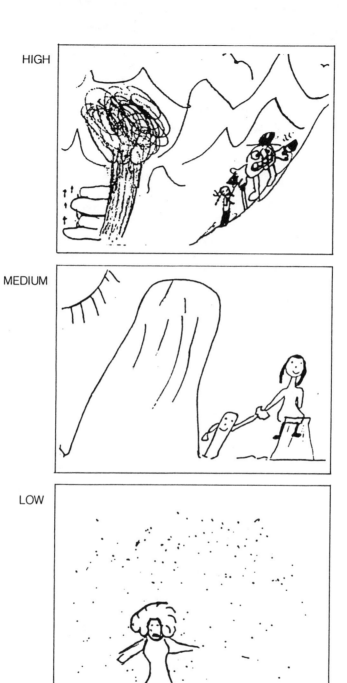

HIGH

MEDIUM

LOW

DRAWING 8   Is the girl crying? Is the Erdluitle holding the cheese and tea? Does he look different from an ordinary human being? Divide and record (see Figure 2–24).

91

Figure 2–25

Drawing 9 for
Erdluitle story: high,
medium, and low
ratings

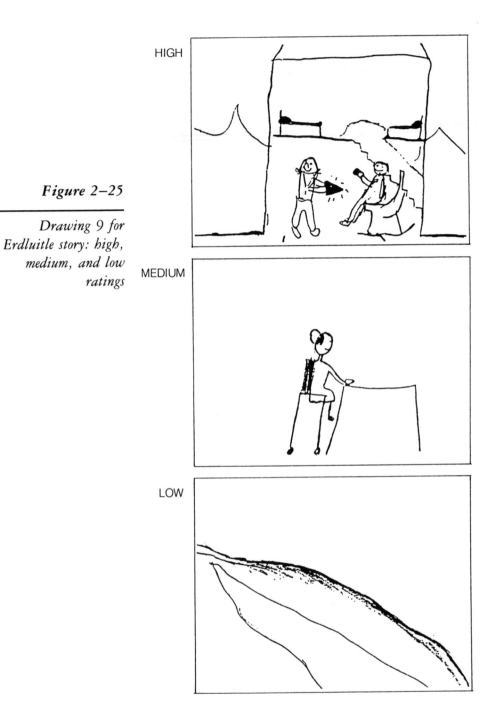

HIGH

MEDIUM

LOW

DRAWING 9   Does the student show the girl's home? Is the student able to show that the mother has gotten well? Does the student show the gold? Divide and record (see Figure 2–25).

92

Figure 2–26

Drawing 10 for Erdluitle story: high, medium, and low ratings

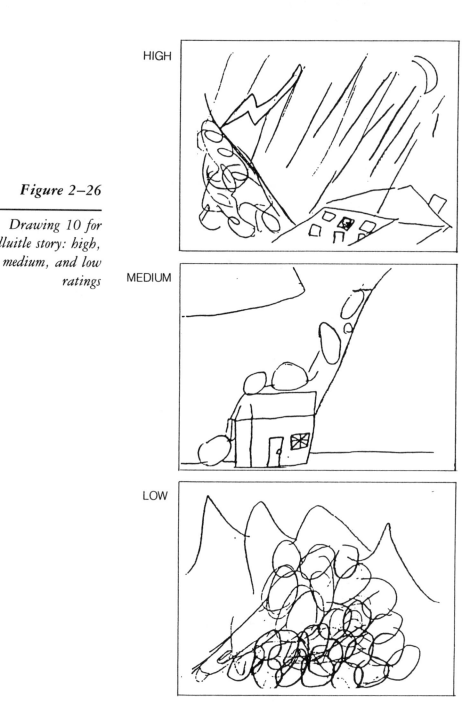

HIGH

MEDIUM

LOW

DRAWING 10 Does the student show that it is night? Does the student show a storm? An avalanche? The miser's house? Divide and record (see Figure 2–26).

93

DRAWING 11   Does the student draw *both* the mother and the daughter? How is peace shown? How does the student convey comfort? Divide and record (see Figure 2–27).

Conclusions   By averaging these pieces of information together, a fairly accurate indication as to the visual-narrative skills of any class can be obtained. These measurements, however, are meant to be only a beginning in the process of observing, identifying, evaluating, and recording the visual-narrative capabilities of students. It is then extremely helpful to compare this information with exercises designed to evaluate the oral and written ability of the same students. Some children will prove to be equally adept using either the visual or verbal mode of expression. This indicates that these children can also benefit from both. Indeed, the students with high verbal abilities are those who function best with traditional types of school instruction. On the other hand, students with higher visual skills will profit most from maximum opportunity in visual exercises combined with the verbal. These are the students most neglected in the traditional classroom settings. Students who are low both verbally and visually will have difficulty in either setting, but these are precisely the students who need optimum attention from both directions, so to speak, and are likely to improve slowly but surely by this complementary approach.

As stated earlier, the typical classroom probably has the following profile, with approximately 25 percent in each category:

a. High verbal and high visual.
b. High verbal and low visual.
c. Low verbal and high visual.
d. Low verbal and low visual.

Once the visual-narrative profile of a class has been established, it can be compared with overall academic performance. Most likely a descending scale, from *a* to *d* will emerge, with *a* being the most successful, and *d* being the least. As a program of visual-narrative drawing becomes fully integrated and firmly established within the language-arts curriculum, however, gradual improvement will be observed, especially in the case of the highly visual child. In sum, the visual learner has everything to gain from an integrated language-arts program.

Figure 2-27

Drawing 11 for Erdluitle story: high, medium, and low ratings

HIGH

MEDIUM

LOW

TEACHING STRATEGIES AND
SUGGESTED ACTIVITIES

*Visual and
Verbal Integration
in the Classroom*

Language-arts teachers can effectively integrate the visual mode of learning into their own curriculum in a variety of ways. The simplest way is by allowing children the opportunity to draw more frequently at all grade levels and to avoid suggesting or implying that such activities are a "waste of time." In contrast, drawing should be looked upon as a way of thinking, a way of knowing, and a valuable tool for the cultivation and expansion of verbal skills. Classroom teachers must engage students in dialogue about what is being drawn. Ask what is happening, and what is going to happen next. Ask students to talk about the characters and the settings of their drawings. Ask about the relationships between characters. Gradually move students into the verbal mode of expression and then ask them to write from their visual stories.

If students cannot think of anything to write, or if they have seemingly exhausted a subject, suggest a series of drawings as a stimulus. If a particular part of a story needs more development, a drawing can be of great help. Visual pictures stimulate reflection and provide the basis for more thought and expression. With a little encouragement and practice, students will soon move easily back and forth between the visual and verbal modes, each mode enhancing and informing the other.

As classroom teachers discover the degree to which this strategy is effective, they will naturally incorporate the visual mode of learning into all areas of their curriculum. It becomes a natural way of thinking for both teacher and student. Teachers will find many ways, through their own experimentation, of integrating the visual-narrative strategy with their own time-tested methods. No longer will the visual be simply tacked on at the end of a lesson to occupy those students who finish an assignment first. It will have an essential place in overall style and planning of all activities.

The following are suggested lessons for integrating the visual-narrative method of writing into an existing language-arts curriculum. Although teachers will discover many more possibilities, these suggestions provide a way to begin.

"I Can't Think of a Story!"

How many times have teachers heard this expression of frustration from students? Teachers try desperately to give them some good ideas, but nothing seems to spark their imagination. At any age, a student can begin by drawing a picture. The simplest, spontaneous drawing can provide a spark for additional reflection and further development. If a student feels the urge to develop a drawing into a narrative sequence of pictures, provide a 9″ × 12″ piece of drawing paper folded into four parts as described previously. The student can continue the sequence in as many spaces as necessary. The student can then write a brief paragraph about each illustration. When the story is finished, sit down and encourage the student to verbalize the pertinent information in each drawing. Engage in dialogue by asking open-ended questions, such as "Why does she look so frightened?" or "What time of day is this happening?" Pause occasionally to ask whether or not the student has included all the visual information into the written version. Very often much is neglected. Teachers can extract this information by asking leading questions that focus on certain details of the drawings. Additional ideas and details can be added to both the verbal and the visual versions of the story, for one always informs the other. But teachers must be very careful not to interpret the drawings themselves. They should not say what *they* think a student is communicating in a drawing, for this would defeat the strategy entirely. What an adult sees in the drawing may not have been the intention of the student at all. The child may, however, be too timid or insecure to contradict the teacher, in which case the authentic meaning is lost. Therefore, be a good listener by raising the kinds of questions that will clarify and help the student to verbalize, but above all pose questions that students can answer for themselves.

Character and Setting Development

This exercise can be done individually or with an entire class. It can be repeated often by merely changing the subject.

Instruct students to fold a piece of 9″ × 12″ drawing paper in half. The paper can be used in either direction, vertically or horizontally. On half of the paper students are asked to draw a picture of a person, animal, or place that could later become part of a story. Shortly after students begin the drawing, suggest that they make a list of words on the other half of the paper—words that they think of as they are drawing. Any word that relates to the drawing is permissible. The list should grow as the drawing develops. Students will need to be reminded often to add to their list. This is particularly true of visual children who become completely absorbed in their drawing. Nevertheless, this transfer from the visual to the verbal is an essential part of the process. It is also visual evidence for the teacher that this translation is, in fact, taking place.

When both the drawing and the list of words are complete, instruct students to finish the exercise by writing about the person, animal, or setting they have just drawn by using many of the words from their list. As they write, new ideas and insights can be added to either the drawing or the writing as they proceed. In fact, it should be encouraged. It is precisely this kind of expansion of description and meaning that is the purpose of this exercise (see Figure 2–28).

The Too-Short   There are always students who insist that they have said everything
Story   they have to say in just a few short sentences. Getting them to say more feels like trying to draw water out of a stone!

Again, they should be instructed to fold a 9″ × 12″ piece of drawing paper into four parts, placing either a key phrase or a sentence from their short story at the bottom of each section. Students should then draw a related picture with as much detail as they can muster. Additional pieces of paper could also be provided in order to list descriptive words as in the previous example. This strategy usually leads to a dramatic expansion of the story.

Selective Expansion   Some stories are long and rather complex but neglect to expand what appears to be a most significant part. By bracketing this portion of the work, the student can easily focus on the problem area by drawing a picture, thus expanding and enhancing the section with more visual information. The student should be asked questions about the drawing in order to facilitate the translation of meaning. By envisioning the incomplete section, the student finds new possibilities that can be translated into written form and thereby complete the story.

An example of this strategy occurred in a fourth-grade class. Rachel was struggling to write her autobiography, and her teacher required

pain
scared
shivery
afual
shakey
fright
feeliny blue
nevouse
feel like scream-
ing

EEk! I skreched when the nurse stuck a needle in my arm.
   I felt pain when the nurse gave me a shot. It felt as if she had shot me with
gine! I could have died!
   "That did'nt hurt did it"? said the nurse "of course" I replied! "You were
just a bit scared" she answered. Boy was she right, I was scared half to
death!
   I was even noevouse (nervous) when Mrs. Miller told me to go to the nurse
because I knew I was going to get a shot.
   I thought I should have been absent but I knew I had already gotten the
shot so I had nothing to worry about.

Figure 2–28

*Drawing, list of
words, and verbal
story*

that all paragraphs should include more than one sentence. But her
second paragraph was only one sentence long: "After I was born my
grandmother and grandfather came to help take care of me." She tried
and tried, but couldn't think of anything else to write. I asked if she
remembered where her grandparents took care of her, and she began
to describe her room. I asked if she could draw a picture. With little
effort she drew a detailed image (see Figure 2–29). When she finished,
I asked her to tell me about her drawing. After verbalizing the details
of her drawing, she was able to write the following paragraph. In fact,
it became the longest paragraph in her story.

Figure 2–29

"After I was born my grandmother and grandfather came to help take care of me"

After I was born my grandmother and grandfather came to help take care of me. The stars were out and the moon was gleaming. It was twelve o'clock that night and I started screaming. My grandmother turned the doorknob and tiptoed into my room. I probably didn't notice her because I was so upset. She saw me all wet because I was crying. I was throwing a temper tantrum! My arms and legs were hitting the mattress. My grandmother picked me up and talked to me to calm me down. After a few minutes I calmed down and stopped crying. My grandmother was good to me.

Sentence Building   Many students have great difficulty constructing sentences that are sufficiently descriptive to say what they mean. Provide such students with a variety of colored pencils. Instruct them to begin drawing with one color only. When a small section is done, they should use the same colored pencil and write a short sentence that describes their drawings. Choosing a different colored pencil, they should add something more to their drawings and then write a second sentence incorporating the new information. This procedure should be repeated with a third, fourth, fifth color, and so on, with each new and more elaborate sentence listed under the previous one. When the sentences become too awkward and cumbersome, the students should stop. The final sentence should be sufficiently descriptive as well as being grammatically correct. The list of sentences will be color-coded, providing both the teacher and the student with the visual source and sequence of this information. This activity could also be done with a team of two to four students, each taking a turn adding a piece to the picture. The construction of the sentences could be a collaborative effort, with each student approving the sentence before it is finalized (see Figure 2–30).

Figure 2–30

Sentence building

- The bug is crawling.
- The plant is shading the bug which is crawling.
- The plant is shading the bug which is crawling on the dirt.
- The bug is being shaded by the plant while another bug crawls closer.
- The bug is being shaded by the plant, while the worm and the bug crawl closer.
- In the terraim box the bug is being shaded by the plant, while the worm and the bug crawl closer.
- David looks into the terraim box while the bug is being shaded by the plant, while the worm and the bug crawl closer.
- David and Matt are looking into the terraim box while the bug is being shaded by the plant, while the worm and the bug crawl closer.

Drawing a Picture Together   There are always some children who lack confidence in drawing as well as writing. An enjoyable way to spark their imaginations is to turn the difficulty into a visual game. The teacher begins by taking a 12″ × 18″ piece of drawing paper and drawing a simple face anywhere on the paper. Ask the students, "Who could this person be?" When they suggest a possibility, ask them to draw what the rest of the person might look like. If the students cannot think of an answer, let them choose from some possibilities the teacher suggests, such as father, doctor, clown, spaceman, and so forth. The students' "turn" should be as long as possible—encourage them to draw as many details as they can think of. It is the teacher's responsibility to ask leading questions, but not to dictate possibilities. Such questions might be: "Where is he?" "Is he alone?" "What is she going to do?" "What time

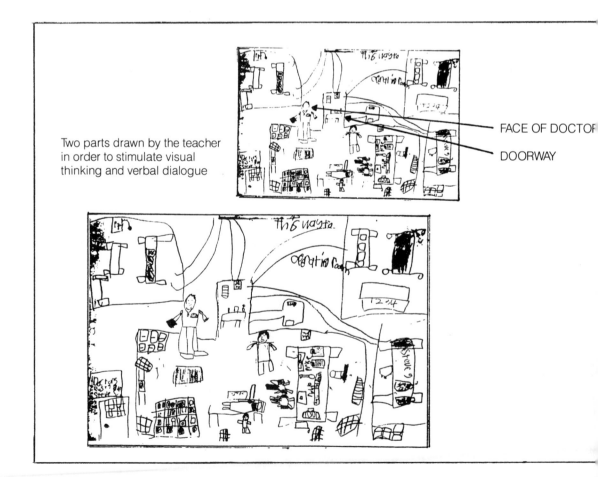

Two parts drawn by the teacher in order to stimulate visual thinking and verbal dialogue

FACE OF DOCTOR

DOORWAY

of year is it?" "How old is she?" and so forth. When the students run out of ideas for the picture, the teacher takes another turn by adding another small detail that may provoke their imagination further, such as a clock on the wall, a window, a mouse in the corner, or raindrops. Do not worry about whether these drawings are well executed. It is the communication between the teacher and the students, and the students with themselves, that is important. In fact, the students may be intimidated if the teacher's drawings are done too well.

Figure 2–31

Drawing a picture together

When the drawing paper is filled with details, the students should be asked to translate the visual information in the drawing into a written story. Because the dialogue and translation take place simultaneously with the act of drawing, the student should be able to proceed easily with the task of writing (see Figure 2–31).

This is the busy office of Dr. Feldman and others. The kid was four years old and his name was Mark. Mark was jumping off his bed. All of a sudden he slipped and broke his arm! "Ding! Ding!" "Yes, this is Dr. Feldman." "Will you send an ambulance to house 35 Wall Street?"

This boy didn't know what was going on! He was as happy as ever until he saw the stretcher. He ran outside and said "You're not taking my mother away from me!" "Correction, we're taking YOU away from your mother. Get in this nice bed." "Okay." Strat, strap, click, click! Meanwhile, "Where is that kid?" Here he is. Dr. Feldman called the nurse.

CHAPTER 2 AT THE HOSPITAL

"What happened?" The mother explained. Next they took x-rays. Then Dr. Feldman said he had a broken arm. WHAT! "Oday, I'll sent others to check. Yup he does, Mrs. Smith. Oh no! I am over time! Len, take cre of Mark. I have to take care of the new born baby."

CHAPTER 3

While Dr. Feldman and Dr. Donoff were taking care of the baby, Dr. Goldberg was talking to Mrs. Smith. Dr Schneider was getting the cast materials ready. Then Dr. Feldman said, "Goodbye. Wait! you forgot your wrist band."

THE END

Everyone Begins with a Drawing

A writing assignment for an entire class can begin with everyone drawing a picture on the same topic. Indeed, "imagining" what to write about is really "imaging" something in visual language. The speed with which individual children are able to move from the visual to the verbal image is a matter of individual differences and learning styles. Beginning a writing lesson with a drawing aids this transfer in the most basic sense. Possible subjects for this exercise could be the circus, colonial America, the airport, or the supermarket (see Figure 2–32.) When all students have completed as detailed a drawing of the subject as possible, they should then make a list of words related to their drawing on a separate piece of paper. From their personal lists, a class list of words can be compiled. Each student can then write a story related to his or her own drawing using any of the words from the class list.

Definitions

Words can be defined either by putting them into a sentence or by illustrating them in a picture. Students should develop a vocabulary notebook that includes both pictures and words. A teacher once told me that if a child can draw the definition of a word, it is more likely to be completely understood and more naturally used within the structure of a written sentence (see Figure 2–33).

Poetry

Poetry lends itself to the visual more than any other kind of writing. This is probably why Archibald MacLeish once said, "A poem should not mean but be." Beautiful lines like the lines of a lovely sunset should not be tampered with and manipulated but enjoyed as they are. Very frequently students ask, after drawing a picture of which they are especially proud, whether it is permissible to write about it in the form of a poem. This kind of translation is very appropriate and should be encouraged. Some students even weave the drawing and the writing together, making an integrated image (see Figure 2–34).

Observation Books

Although students enjoy writing and drawing fiction, they should also have many opportunities to write descriptively and analytically about everyday occurrences in their lives. Two problems are particularly prominent with this kind of writing:

Figure 2–32

Classroom drawings on one topic of the circus

TRAIN

STRIKE

BELT

Figure 2–33

Definitions

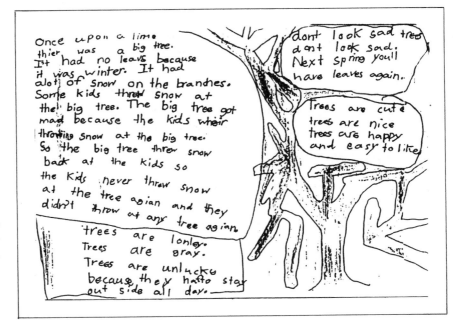

Figure 2–34

Drawing and writing to express winter trees

1. Children don't think they do anything worth writing about. They often think that everything they write should be an adventure story or a fairy tale.
2. In the attempt to make a rather mundane description more exciting, they run many events together to make it seem long but neglect to bring out the details about particular events.

If children can be taught to be better observers, they will become better writers. Thus the use of "observation books" can be a great assistance in helping children to really "see" their everyday activities.

Provide each student with a small 6″ × 9″ book with blank, unlined pages and a spiral binding. They are normally called sketch books, but "observation books" is a better name because the purpose is then clear to all, especially if the books are purchased by principals or parents. Instruct students to draw a specific number of pictures in their books each week. Two to four drawings seem to be a reasonable number. Listing words at the edges of each drawing could also be suggested, especially for the students who have difficulty writing.

The observation book becomes a reference for possible writing projects that are descriptive or analytical in nature. Whenever students can't think of something to write about, they should refer to their observation books. They will soon have a surplus of subject matter, such as playing hockey, getting a shot from the nurse, helping mother fix dinner, playing Monopoly with the family, practicing the piano, and so on. Indeed, the personal history recorded in these observation books will provide a wealth of information and details of events (preserved in picture form) that would otherwise be forgotten. Each drawing contains the potential for inspiring a personal piece of writing.

Slide Tapes   Photographing a sequence of drawings in slide form provides a variety of possibilities. A number of pictures that together tell a story can then be projected in sequence. The student can tape-record a verbal narrative to accompany the visual narrative. The student could also write dialogue and direct a group of students to play the roles of the characters in the story. Sound effects could also be included. Children take great delight in presenting the finished slide tape to an audience of peers and/or adults.

Visual Arts   Most school systems provide special instruction in the visual arts. What students are doing in their art classes can provide motivation for excellent language-arts activities and should therefore be of great interest to all teachers of the language arts. The art curriculum is designed to engage students in imaginative and creative thinking. Drawings, paintings, sculptures, prints, murals, and collages also have rich and varied narrative potential. Language-arts teachers should therefore establish a close relationship with the teacher in their school who is a specialist in the visual arts. Such a move would demonstrate a genuine interest for all students, as well as show a deeper understanding for the relationship between the visual and the verbal dimensions of experience, expression, meaning, and above all, learning. It should always be remembered, however, that the translation from the visual to the verbal mode does not happen automatically. It is the responsibility of the language-arts teacher to facilitate this process, for only under the guidance of an informed, sensitive, respectful, and patient teacher will all children be able to reach their full potential.

CHAPTER 3

THE SPECIAL-EDUCATION PROGRAM

Special-education programs generally serve the needs of children who are considered to be "different" or "abnormal" (Ysseldyke and Algozzine, 1984, 4). It is generally believed that these children cannot realize their full educational potential in a regular classroom. These children could be physically handicapped, emotionally disturbed, mentally retarded, learning disabled, or even gifted and talented.

I am primarily concerned with the student who is categorized as "learning disabled." So many children have been categorized at such an astonishing rate during the past decade that some states have estimated that 15 percent of their students can be so labeled (Coles, 1987, 10). Between 1976 and 1983, the number of children classified as learning disabled increased from 800,000 to 1.8 million (Coles, 205). This large increase has led to a national shortage of special-education teachers and is the source of an educational dilemma and controversy. The area of learning disabilities did not even exist before 1960, and it now accounts for approximately 40 percent of all special-education programs.

Who are the learning disabled, and why are their numbers growing? They are predominantly male, of middle-class background, and have relatively well-educated parents. Their IQs are normal, but their reading, writing, and spelling abilities run at least two years behind those of other children of the same age. They are often daydreamers, have a hard time focusing on academic material, have a hard time sitting still, and often suffer from low self-esteem. These students cause classroom teachers and parents much anxiety and anguish, and parents and teachers frequently hold each other responsible for the children's poor behavior and/or low academic achievement.

Since there have always been so called "slow" and "underachieving" children, even in "the good old days," how then did the learning disability phenomenon get started? Gerald Coles (1987) explains:

> First and foremost in explaining the sudden emergence of LD
> [Learning Disabilities] is the "unexpected" and seemingly
> unexplainable academic failure of many middle-class children (in
> contrast to the "explainable" failure of many "disadvantaged"
> children). This failure grew from and contrasted with another
> aspect of the current social context, the postwar prosperity,

which had led middle-class parents to anticipate continued if not improved success for their children. This expectation was fueled by the belief, partly factual and partly ideological, that education would be *the* vehicle for individual success. And the atmosphere of protest in the 1960s led to demands for the reform of many social institutions, particularly the schools. The LD field was significantly shaped by the federal government's attempt to assuage social discontent and by the ways in which social institutions, and especially the schools, "allowed" reform to occur. (24)

From the parent's perspective, the term *learning disabled* did not carry the negative connotation that *retarded* or *emotionally disturbed* did, and yet their child would be eligible to receive the special help and attention they felt was necessary. For them, no stigma was attached to the label, for they were in no way at fault.

With more and more children being classified as learning disabled, it is reasonable to ask, "What is being done for them?" and "Is it working?" The field of special education has been given an enormous responsibility. Because special education is a helping profession, with caring and well-meaning professionals doing the very best they can, it is not easy to be critical of it. As one teacher expressed it, "My own effectiveness will ultimately be measured in terms of the number of children 'out' of special programs . . . as compared to the numbers 'in' " (Ysseldyke & Algozzine, 1984, 24).

Unfortunately, the numbers are growing rather than declining. Something is just not working! Why? What is the field of special education doing or not doing that is making this program so ineffective? Or is the source of the problem somewhere outside the field, with special education actually being the victim? In order to search for some answers, consider two crucial areas of the field—clinical research and classroom pedagogy.

First of all, clinical research has been operating on what I consider a basically faulty premise—that something is "wrong" with the child. Consequently, such research teams have more or less gone on a wild goose chase looking for the defective part. But after searching for decades, they have found absolutely nothing to support this thesis!

In their search, clinicians first looked at the brain for the source of the problem.

> The brain damage theory, or minimal brain dysfunction (MBD) hypothesis, has been developed from the following rationale: If a child has difficulty learning to read, shows confusion in the visual orientation of symbols, and/or fails to grasp the phonetic structure of the alphabet (which leads to bizarre spelling mistakes), *or*, in the case of the hyperactive child, consistently fails to behave properly in the classroom, something must be wrong with the child's brain. Because the deficit is so situation-specific, the brain damage theory adds the corollary that as nothing appears to be amiss with the child's spoken language or general intelligence, then the brain damage must be "minimal." When any term such as "minimal" ("ideopathic," "essential," and "primary" are a few others) is used in medicine, it not only means that there is no valid diagnosis, but it also means that clinicians haven't the vaguest notion of where or what such tissue damage might be. When attempts are made to discover differences between normal children and those with specific learning problems by various types of neurological tests, nothing can be found. Yet the theory still persists despite the lack of hard evidence. (McGuinness, 1985, 36)

The possibility of some kind of visual or perceptual problem has also been explored as the possible source. Motivated by such problems as word-blindness and dyslexia, research has still not been able to produce any hard evidence to prove that children with such problems do not see in the same way as so-called normal children. It is interesting to note that many artists and art students are in fact dyslexic in a field that requires a high degree of perceptual acuity.

Researches have also looked for the answer to the dilemma within the family structure of the learning-disabled student. Some have concluded that whatever is "wrong" must be inherited because it seems to run in families; others contend that families are probably to blame because they don't seem to read to their children enough or language is not a high priority with such families. This of course does not explain why one learning-disabled child might have "normal" siblings.

In the case of hyperactivity and attention-deficit disorder, many possible causes have been scrutinized as the possible cause. Analysis of such things as body chemicals, brain waves (EEG), heart rates, and skin conductance levels have all been studied, but have resulted in no conclusive evidence of anything being "wrong" with the learning-disabled child.

It seems strange that because the disability is a language problem, it has been generally accepted that something must be "wrong." If a child cannot learn to draw, play the piano, or dismantle and reassemble an engine, shouldn't he or she also be considered brain damaged? McGuinness (1985) asserts that it is a cultural prejudice that elevates language proficiency to this superior level, that society expects that all human beings should be able to obtain it, and that something is drastically wrong if they can't. McGuinness, on the other hand, contends that perfectly normal brains can be different from one another and that "people can have completely normal brains but still have difficulty in learning to read or fail to concentrate on classroom pursuits" (36).

With the narrow focus of such research dominating the field, what then has been the result in the classroom? How have schools responded to these children? What curricular and pedagogical decisions have been made to address the problem of children with so-called learning disabilities?

I have not been able to find any evidence that anything unique is being done for these children in the way of actual instruction. The student may receive more individualized attention, the pace may be slower and the lessons more structured, but otherwise it is simply more of the same—words, words, words, resulting in very little improvement, if any at all. Could it possibly be that many, if not most, of these children are visual learners, and they simply do not respond to the traditional verbal approach to learning?

What *is* unique is the enormous amount of paperwork being generated by this attention as well as the size and growth of bureaucracy in special education. Government regulations have made it necessary for special-education teachers and supervisors to spend an undue amount of time on referrals, evaluations, consultations, court hearings, debates, and so on, all requiring written documentation and classification. By the time a learning-disabled student graduates from high school, his or her educational career is documented in minute detail, much more thoroughly than a "normal" child's, but in most cases he or she will still be left with the same debilitating language problem.

So what should or can be done? First of all, attitudes must change. As long as children who are verbal learners are considered to be "normal" and visual learners abnormal, the problem will persist. This is not to suggest that *all* learning-disabled children are visual learners. Certainly there are those who have something organically "wrong" with them. Neurophysiological researches on so-called defective parts should continue. But other avenues should also be explored. The possibility that some children are simply "different" from others and still "normal" should be seriously considered. This point of view would allow for a variety of strengths and weaknesses in aptitudes, including language proficiency. Only then will significant insight occur and the word people who dominate the profession no longer be allowed to overlook the unique strengths of the visual learner. Teaching strategies could be initiated in regular classroom settings, which would eliminate the necessity for referring large numbers of children to special education. Those in the field would be able to concentrate on the smaller percentage of students who are indeed "abnormal." By focusing on and succeeding in helping those students, they would significantly reduce their feelings of being frustrated and overwhelmed by an impossible task.

BECOMING INFORMED

At a recent conference titled "Learning Disabled Children *Can* Write!" (Teachers College, Columbia University, February 21, 1987), four speakers, all specialists in the field, noted that many of their students had above-average drawing ability. But this ability was mentioned only as an interesting characteristic rather than a clue to the problem.

One teacher who works at a school specializing in students with learning disabilities made some comments that were of particular concern. He described the writing program in grades one through eight at his school, and during his presentation, he discussed the case of Adam, one of his students. He showed some examples of Adam's very elaborate and detailed narrative drawings. At last, it seemed, a teacher of words who recognized the importance and the potential of a student's visual ability. Unfortunately, he was showing the drawings simply to illustrate his own personal goal. "I want Adam to be as expressive in his writing as he is in his drawings," he explained. It still seemed as though he understood until he elaborated further: "But getting him not to draw, not to fiddle around is sometimes difficult. Drawing *after* writing is fine, but I discourage it *before* writing!" To my utter amazement, several teachers in the audience got up and confirmed that this indeed was a problem they also had.

All too often, such students are given only token recognition of their visual ability, with the offhand comment, "Isn't it nice [he or she] can do something well?" But sometimes they are not even given that much recognition.

One day in the teacher's room, I overheard a conversation between a school psychologist and a special-education teacher. They were discussing Jonathan, a thirteen-year-old mildly retarded or severely learning-disabled student. The psychologist summarized his opinion: "He has absolutely no strengths, no strengths whatsoever!" His teacher agreed. I felt compelled to enter the conversation by asking, "But have you ever seen Jonathan's drawings? He draws very well!" The psychologist looked as though I were out of my mind, and without so much as a reply, he looked at his watch and said, "I have to get going." He promptly closed his briefcase and left. He was not interested and never pursued the matter further.

It was true that Jonathan had very few strengths, but to say he had none was simply not true. He spent several hours a day watching cartoons on television. He could reproduce a likeness of any cartoon character he had seen. He had a very good visual memory. After I discussed this ability with his teacher, she began to realize that it was also true in other areas. He could remember descriptive details, for example, that others had difficulty remembering, such as the license-plate number of a motorcycle he had seen on the way to school, or the color of cars belonging to teachers parked in the parking lot. Jonathan's visual memory was indeed his "strength" (see Figures 3–1 through 3–8).

I believe the examples of Adam and of Jonathan are not unusual, but are instead rather typical. They unfortunately illustrate a severe lack of sensitivity and understanding by the professionals who should be better informed. Recognizing and understanding the needs of the visual learner is necessary, if students such as Adam and Jonathan are to be well served by our departments of special education and our public schools.

FLINTSTONES
CHARACTERS

FRED FLINTSTONE'S CAR

Figure 3–1

*Cartoon characters
drawn by Jonathan
from memory*

SNOOPY

Figure 3–2

*Visual expression
of a name*

Figure 3–3

*A visual story about
creatures from space*

Figure 3-4

A close-up sequence

Figure 3–5

"Kermit the Frog"

KERMIT THE FROG*

I'm walking down the side walk and I'm going through the garage door into my house. My nephew Herman Kermit Junior, the frog, is visiting me. I live on Washington Street. There's a meautiful sunset. It is a cold, but beautiful day.

*Jonathan composed this sensitive visual and verbal story about the Kermit the Frog puppet he received for his birthday.

Figure 3–6

Love, hearts, and marriage

"This drawing is about love, hearts and my sister's marriage. My sister and my brother-in-law are standing in their kitchen."

Bad Sam pushed good Henry out into space because he din't like him. He does't like anything that's good. Sam's brain got damaged and that made him angry, and that made him bad. Henry is good because he's happy. He's happy because he got a new car.

Good Henry would go home and tell his parents. His parents would go and tell bad Sam's parents. They would make an agreement to be friends. Both boys would become half good and half bad. This is the only way they can be friends.

This very touching and revealing narrative was first expressed visually. The verbal narrative was then dictated.

Figure 3–8

Self-portrait

Figure 3–7

A two-part narrative

THEORETICAL IMPLICATIONS FOR VISUAL AND VERBAL LEARNERS

CHAPTER 4

HISTORICAL GROUNDS FOR TEACHING WRITING THROUGH VERBAL AND VISUAL MODES OF EXPRESSION

Educators seem to ask the same questions decade after decade: "Why can't Johnny read?" and "Why can't Johnny write?" Why do some children have so much difficulty learning to use the English language? Education history suggests that students can improve their language skills through a method of instruction that facilitates a transfer of meaning between the visual and the verbal modes of expression.

In 1892, frustrated Harvard composition teachers asked, "Why can't Harvard's entering freshmen write clearly in their mother tongue?" (Jackson, 1986, 601). They complained: "It would certainly seem not unreasonable to insist that young men nineteen years of age who present themselves for a college education should be able not only to speak, but to write their mother tongue with ease and correctness" (601). In 1911, at the first meeting of the National Council of Teachers of English, the "chaotic condition" of elementary school English was bemoaned (Hook, 1986, 538). In 1971, the Growth and Development Branch of the National Institute of Child Health and Human Development held a conference to try to understand better why so many children who can listen and speak so well should find it so very difficult to read and write (Kavanagh & Mattingly, 1972). And in 1986, the teaching of writing was featured in a special "Campus" issue of *Newsweek* magazine. Such attention given to this problem over the years suggests that something is seriously wrong with educational practice.

Educators generally accept the fact that children are not the same in other respects, such as athletic ability or singing ability. Why are these same educators blind to the fact that some children need a more visual approach to help them learn to write? Either they don't believe it or they don't understand it. Given the modern emphasis upon the achievement of mass literacy, understanding basic differences between children becomes a very serious matter indeed. Parents accuse educators of not doing their jobs properly; legislatures and school committees introduce minimum competency tests; some authorities, such as Rudolf Flesch (1955, 1981), scream for "back to basics"; and still others advocate more experimentation. And as a by-product of all this tremendous pressure, additional anxiety and frustration are heaped high upon the heads of the little Johnnys who can't or won't read and/or write.

The question of Why? continues to be asked, and the answer continues to elude inquirers. Perhaps we can find the answer by looking at two important sources of information: the history of our own written language and the children themselves. By studying both very carefully, it becomes clear that children acquire writing skills very similarly to the way written language developed historically.

THE HISTORICAL DEVELOPMENT OF WRITING AND ITS RELATION TO CHILDREN

The success story of phonetic scripts spans the past five thousand years. But sometimes with great achievement comes great loss, and what has been lost in the history of writing is its visual, or pictorial, aspect (see Figure 4–1). In order then to envision writing, we must first see how it has been de-visualized to the point that there is—as with the printed letters on this page—absolutely no visual correspondence whatsoever between words and what they signify. For example, the word *dog* does not look like a dog. In order to appreciate fully the significance of this progressive effacement of the visual from writing, we must also ask: Was it inevitable that this effacement should take place? And if it was inevitable, why did it not happen more uniformly throughout the world, especially in Eastern scripts? Or is it precisely the persistence of the visual in Chinese and Japanese that led the famous father of modern linguistics, Ferdinand de Saussure (1966), to observe that there are two fundamentally different types of writing: (a) writing that is a substitute for discourse, and (b) writing that is a second kind of language?

Phonetical writing is the discourse type, and pre-(or only partially) phoneticized writing is the latter type. So it is, Saussure suggests, that the Chinese or Japanese person writing in traditional characters, when uncertain as to the meaning of something, may jot down a few characters to "see" what he means. But in this case "seeing what he means" is not just a metaphoric expression (as we might say, "How can I know what I mean until I see what I've said?"). In highly pictorial systems such as Chinese and Japanese, an actual visual correspondence exists between what is written and the reality to which it points. But just how did this complete effacement of the visual actually take place in Western scripts? The key, according to I. M. Gelb (1952), lies in the transition from pictorial prewriting systems to fully phoneticized

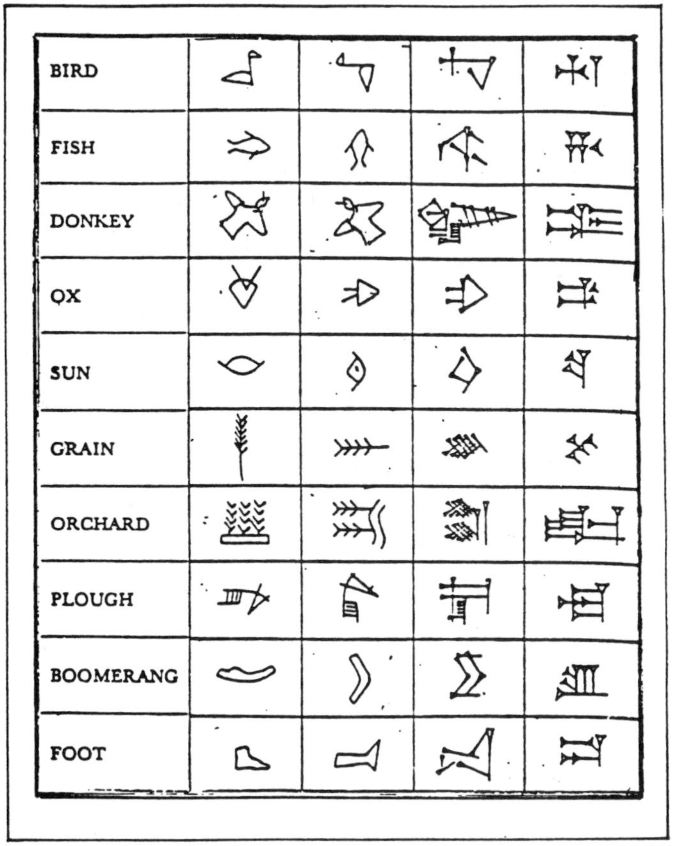

Figure 4–1

Pictorial origin of ten cuneiform signs (Gelb, 1952, 70)

systems. The pre-writing systems included the picture and the *logogram*, (a symbol for naming objects, number, proper names, geographic locations, and the like), as well as picture writing, using a single symbol to represent the many meanings of a given word. For example, in Summerian script an arrow could represent *arrow* as well as the homonym *life*. The use of homonyms made it possible for people to communicate deeper concepts with the same symbols (Gelb, 1952). It was only when whole-word signs for word meaning became cumbersome and confusing that word symbols began to represent equivalent syllables, followed by signs representing individual syllables.

The biggest leap occurred about five thousand years ago with the emergence of the great Oriental systems—the Summerian, Egyptian,

Hittite, and Chinese word-syllabic systems. This giant step represented the beginning of phonetical representation. The total victory of phonetization, of course, came with the Greek alphabet—the Greeks chose to represent each spoken sound with a symbol (or letter). But what is most important about this transition is that all of these writing forms and systems were originally picture drawings. Because phonetical representation was viewed as an important advancement, the significant roll the picture played in this achievement often went unnoticed. Just as speech developed out of the imitation of sound, writing developed out of the imitation of forms of real objects or beings. At the beginning of all writing stands the picture (Gelb, 1952).

The picture also constitutes the beginning of the child's written language. Just as all written language evolved from or in partnership with the picture, so too children develop a mastery of written language by integrating their pictures and their words. One informs the other. Contrary to Eric Havelock (1976), who asserted that the perfected written language would be comparable to an electric current that instantly reaches the brain, it may be that the goal of written language is to retain and even augment the visual element—not to eliminate it. We may have something to learn from the Chinese and the Japanese, in this regard, as to the possible benefits of retaining the visual element.

Chinese calligraphy has a logical structure of its own based upon the logical structure of pictorial objects; once a pictogram was established, it conveyed a clear meaning that even children could understand. The transition from the pure pictogram to the ideogram (idea or concept) and the phonogram (sound) occurred later, allowing for more subtleties in definition. This development was a gradual process similar to the word-building procedures that shaped Western languages. For example, pictograms were combined to form ideograms which, in turn, could be used to represent more complex ideas. A sun rising 日 behind a tree 木, brought about the character 東 meaning the direction *east*. A tree 木 doubled 林 formed the character for *forest*, and, if tripled, 森 the character meant *a dense forest*. Similarly, when a new character for *brightness* was needed, it was very natural to combine the two brightest heavenly bodies, the sun and the moon, to form the new character 明.

Word building, however, is not simply a matter of the visual manipulation of the basic pictogram forms. A second method has to do with the formulation of phonograms that consist of two components: the pictogram root called a *radical* (there are some 214 pictogram radicals that provide the basis for the more than 40,000 characters in classical Chinese [Fazzioli, 1987, 14]); and the second phonetic indicator that provides the clue for proper pronunciation. Extending the meaning of a given character did not necessarily require the addition of complex grammatical elements. 日 , meaning *sun*, could mean *day* in another context. 月 , meaning *moon*, could also mean *month* (as it does in North American Indian dialects). Words or characters are thus used to form sentences according to common sense and the logic of the context. The classical Chinese, Korean, and Japanese characters represent root ideas rather than specific parts of speech, as in Western languages. Grammar is much simpler, with no hard and fast rules regarding gender, number, case, tense, and participles.

The calligraphic (meaning "words written by hand") form of these characters is itself a legitimate and widely appreciated visual art form. Calligraphy incorporates all the elements of a painting—line, shape, texture, unity, balance, rhythm, proportion—all within its own unique form of composition. Long (1987) describes how calligraphy expresses both the visual and the verbal modes of thought and communication:

> Lei Chien-Fu once wrote a piece of calligraphy which represented the ebb and flow of the waves in an incoming tide. His inspiration, though made up of words, was in reality an abstract painting. Following the flow of the brush stroke, the twists and turns of the brush, can enable the viewer to enjoy and experience the feelings which the artist has endeavored to express. (36)

It is this unique characteristic of calligraphy that is described by Long as the "visual dimension of thought" (39). Hence it is not surprising that Chinese and other Oriental paintings, in sharp contrast to the Western, should routinely contain calligraphy as an integral part of the composition. For calligraphy is viewed as an essential component of the painting and as being vital to the overall concept of the artist's visual image. This calligraphy may be a poem that evokes in words the story or the mood told by the visual image. The brush strokes of the characters harmonize in style with the brush strokes of the image. The characters provide both an aesthetic and an explanatory dimension to the painting, and this makes the work complete. In the West, by contrast, the writing of words on a canvas is likely to be viewed as a defacement of the work unless the artist happens to be portraying a scene already containing written words, like the page of a book or a street sign.

This ancient Oriental tradition of integrating word and image closely parallels the visual-narrative method of writing proposed in this book. From the Eastern point of view, the separation of the visual form from the verbal is a most unnatural thing to do. Is this the reason so many children have difficulty mastering written language in Western culture? Can it be that the conventions informing our understanding of fully phoneticized scripts are based on assumptions that simply do not hold true in the case of many individuals?

Egon Weigl (1980), for example, points out how difficult the final linguistic leap is for the young child. He explains that nothing we demand of children in the field of reading and writing is in any way organically, emotionally, or rationally connected to previous experiences in their lives. This applies both to grasping the concept of an alphabetical writing system and to learning the specific symbols involved. This process involves a very high level of abstraction, first among all the various aspects of spoken language and also among its many phonological features. At the same time, children have to develop definite analytical synthetic strategies in order to separate the flow of language not only into words and syllables but also into individual sounds. At a very young age, they must also accept, store, and follow what appear to be inconsistencies and unexplainable rules.

According to Dixon (1983), these inconsistencies are especially troublesome for the visual/spatial learner. He explains that because the visual child is primarily a "holistic synthesizer" of information, rather than a "linear processor" (202), great difficulties lead to sequential memory problems of various kinds. And since language proficiency is dependent on proper and correct sequencing, language problems multiply for visual learners. These difficulties are compounded by the numerous inconsistencies within the English language itself. Contrary to what many educators would have us believe, English is not a particularly phonetic language and has many inconsistencies that have to be mastered by memory. Dixon (1983) illustrates the problem by pointing out the following:

> These seven words all rhyme: To, Through, Moo, Two, Grew, Too, True. Yet each contains a different spelling for the same phoneme. As if having seven or more spellings for the same phoneme were not bad enough, the same spelling can be associated with several phonemes. Vowels have several different pronunciations, and even a complex letter group like *ough* is pronounced one way in *through*, another way in *thought*, and still a third way in *enough*. (203)

The visual learner looks for a logical pattern upon which to organize large amounts of data. Mastering these inconsistencies can therefore be extremely stressful and unnatural for this child, especially if the more natural visual element is not encouraged or given the same status that writing skills receive. Teachers and parents should be patient and understanding. After all, the Greeks took thousands of years to take the giant step to a phonetical language. We expect children to make that leap in a few short years. The process should not be rushed.

One might assume at this point that most scholars accept the notion that true writing must, in some degree, be phonetical. But this view has not met with total acceptance. Other scholars, such as the anthropologist Dennis Tedlock (1981), have severely questioned the "phonetic prejudice" of modern linguistics. In addition to his skepticism regarding the adequacy of classifying pre-Columbian pictogram inscriptions as "pre-" or "partial" writing systems, Tedlock reminds us that much of the texture of spoken language is simply lost in phonetization. Fully phoneticized scripts simply cannot capture the subtle nuances, gestures, and other visual and auditory aspects of living discourse. He criticizes the "egocentrism" of modern scholarship, especially as it relates to the study of pre- or only partially literate societies—cultures that live and move in the context of ritual and oral tradition, not in the context of "texts." We must, therefore, question the phonetic prejudice we have inherited—especially its recorded forms—and the assumption that when we have read written words in a text, we have acquired a corresponding reality.

EIGHTEENTH- AND NINETEENTH-CENTURY THEORIES AND PRACTICES: ROUSSEAU, FROEBEL, ALCOTT

For years, psychologists have researched the development of language in children. Classroom pedagogy in American schools has probably been informed most by the work of Jean Piaget and Jerome Bruner. However, I believe that it is the Russian psychologist, L. S. Vygotsky (1978), who most clearly understands the important role of drawing in the development of oral and written speech. Vygotsky, in fact, does not see drawing as separate from speech; he actually regards it as a particular kind of speech in and of itself. Unfortunately, because Vygotsky is unfamiliar to most Western educationists, his unique and important insights have escaped their attention altogether.

Vygotsky considers the *gesture* to be the initial visual sign that contains the child's future writing, just as an acorn contains the future oak tree; he argues that make-believe play and drawing are the connecting link between the gesture and writing. Consider the following scenario described by Judith Burton (1980b):

> Following a class dialogue about the selection and creating of different lines in a painting, five-year-old Rodney picked up his brush, made a line, then announced, "I'm going to make a car, a racing car, to go fast." With great speed, punctuated by an occasional pause for reflection, Rodney made a painting. Before the paint was dry, he sought out his teacher to look at what he had made. "It goes along the tracks, goes along here—brooom brooom; then along here—eeek, eeek; gets faster and faster— eeeow; and goes along here—brooom brooom!" As he explained his painting, Rodney accompanied his words with furious driving gestures, following the twists and bends in the painted lines as if driving along them. (60)

This multifaceted display illustrates most convincingly Vygotsky's belief that such signs—make-believe play and drawing—are, at this point, "first order symbols . . . directly denoting objects or actions, and the child has yet to reach second-order symbolism, which involves the creation of written signs for the spoken symbols as words" (1978, 115). The importance of drawing in the development of language is made clearer in the following statement:

The child must make a basic discovery—namely that one can draw not only things but also speech. It was only this discovery that led humanity to the brilliant method of writing by words and letters; the same thing leads children to letter writing. From the pedagogical point of view, this transition should be arranged by shifting the child's activity from drawing things to drawing speech. It is difficult to specify how this shift takes place, since the appropriate research has yet to lead to definite conclusions, and the generally accepted methods of teaching writing do not permit the observation of it. One thing only is certain—that the written language of children develops in this fashion, shifting from drawings of things to drawing of words . . . the entire secret of teaching written language is to prepare and organize this natural transition appropriately. (115–16)

Although I would argue a bit with Vygotsky regarding the naturalness of this transition (if by "natural" he means automatic or inevitable), the critical point is that Vygotsky sees drawing as an integral part of speech. For Vygotsky, make-believe play, drawing, and writing are "different moments in an essentially unified process" (116) rather than distinctively separate sequential "stages," as in Jerome Bruner's view. If educators, like Vygotsky, recognize and accept the visual component as an integral and necessary part of the evolution of written language, they must then ask if educational theory and/or practice have ever reflected this understanding. To help answer this question, I have selected three theorists and/or practitioners—Jean-Jacques Rousseau, Friedrich Froebel, and Amos Bronson Alcott—whose insights and strategies are worth discussing in some detail.

Jean-Jacques Rousseau (1712–78)

Rousseau's treatise *Emile* was first published in 1762, causing controversy across Europe and ultimately beyond. In this book, he presented a revolutionary view of the child, of educational practice, and of the student-teacher relationship. Rousseau's understanding of the child came from observing nature, unfolding and blossoming according to its own innate timetable, and he concluded that the child, an issue of nature, will learn what he or she needs to learn and should therefore never be rushed. He explains that it is nature that provides the master plan for the child's growth and development, and it should in no way be interfered with or severe problems will result. The child's natural instincts and desires should be respected: "Let them run, jump and shout to their hearts' content" (1984, 50). Statements such as this caused the uproar.

In spite of his brash and rather arrogant manner, there is more than a little truth to many of Rousseau's statements, especially in light of what we know of current classroom practice. Today all children *must* learn to read and write when they are six years old. Imagine how the parents of a future Harvard graduate would respond to Rousseau's views:

> What we are in no hurry to get is usually obtained with speed and certainty. I am pretty sure Emile will learn to read and write before he is ten, just because I care very little whether he can do so before he is fifteen; but I would rather he never learnt to read at all, than that his art should be acquired at the price of all that makes reading useful. What is the use of reading to him if he always hates it? (1984, 81–82)

Observing the child's natural instincts, Rousseau encouraged Emile to draw from nature. He was confident that by observing and drawing the real world, the boundless world of the imagination would gradually open up. Rousseau regarded drawing as a vital part of a child's education and obviously understood its unique relationship to the child's language development. He simply stated, "All languages are the result of {this} art" (32).

Rousseau criticized education that relied predominately on words: "Thoughts are not in his tongue, but in his brain" (124). The word-oriented system of education we have today does not take its clues from the child or from nature; it demonstrates an impatience with the natural order and the natural evolution of learning.

Rousseau's statements seem especially relevant today for the child who is "naturally" visual rather than verbal. John Dixon (1983), who has recently described the problem of motivation for spatial children, seems to echo Rousseau's concern:

> Unlike many other children, they have little motivation to pursue language study for its own sake. Being inclined to take in the full sensory depth and breadth of the world around them, the

very idea of spending hours scanning with one's eyes along rows of small black shapes called letters is antithetical to what life is about for these children. . . . to narrow one's sensory field of intake to such boring "book-scapes" causes the child to meander in his reading behavior and to fill his mind with interesting daydreams far removed from the content of the reading. Failure to tie language learning to the things that are fascinating to the child are bound to render all other technically grounded teaching relatively ineffective. (197)

This is the child to whom Rousseau would pay attention: "Teach your [student] the phenomena of nature; you will soon rouse his curiosity. . . . but if you would have it grow, do not be in too great a hurry" (131).

Friedrich Froebel *(1782–1852)* In contrast to Rousseau, Friedrich Froebel's theories of education were widely accepted in both Europe and the United States. Widely known as the "father of the kindergarten," Froebel proposed a theory of "inner connectedness." He (1974) understood that the child's drawing is the connecting link between word and object and that it is also *equal* to the word:

The drawing properly stands between the word and the thing, shares certain qualities with each of them, and is therefore, so valuable in the development of the child. The true drawing has this in common with the thing, that it seeks to represent it in form and outline; like the word, however, it never is the thing itself, but only an image of the thing. The word and the drawing are again clearly opposed in their nature: for the drawing is dead, while the word lives; the drawing is visible, as the word is audible. The word and the drawing, therefore, belong together inseparable, as light and shadow, night and day, soul and body do. (79)

The natural connectedness between drawing and writing is evident historically and in the development of children:

Both the pictorial (hieroglyphics) and alphabetic (conventional letters) writing imply an exceedingly rich life—only out of this richness writing was born. (Froebel, 1974, 221)

In children we see the inner desire for both symbolic and pictorial writing. (223)

Thus, the *art of writing* is developed in each individual human being in the general historical way and in agreement with the general course of development of the human mind. (221)

Froebel (1974) hoped to accomplish "inner connectedness" by encouraging children to motivate themselves, thereby unfolding their own willpower:

> Each successive generation and each successive individual human being, inasmuch as he would understand the past and present, must pass through all preceding phases of human development and culture, and this should not be done in the way of dead imitation or mere copying, but in the way of living, spontaneous self-activity. (17–18)

Drawing was highly regarded by Froebel because it stemmed from a basic inner need of the child. Froebel lamented, however, that this view was not widely accepted:

> It is in drawing that the child pre-eminently shows himself to be creative because with limited control of the material and with little physical effort he can recognizably show what he wants to express. Yet so far drawing has not been generally regarded as essential, and as a result children have been deprived of one of the most effective means of their education. (Lilley, 1967, 115)

Froebel recognized that schools placed a much higher value on words:

> In the out-leading processes of intellectual growth, in the expression of ideas, the school is still satisfied with words and ignores the value of things; it recognizes the debt of gratitude the intellect owes to the reflex influence which comes from efforts to formulate knowledge in words, but neglects that plastic expression of ideas by the hands which hold to their formulation in words the same relation that things hold to symbols in impression. (37)

Fortunately, Froebel's theories of education were widely accepted and spawned the great kindergarten movement of the late nineteenth century. His theories concerning drawing and writing, however, were not incorporated into the curriculum beyond first grade. Education primarily by words alone would set the standard.

Amos Bronson Alcott (1799–1888)

Bronson Alcott was more of a teacher than a theorist. He actually practiced what he believed in the classroom. He stood unique among his peers, because he understood that a good education is not achieved by words alone. The method of "imaging" that he integrated into his curriculum was unique for his times and, so it seems, for any time since. In part because of his individualism, he was vastly misunderstood and unappreciated. Even today, Alcott is regarded no more than a minor figure in the historical literature of American education. The value he accorded to imaging or visual thinking set him against the mainstream direction of educational practice.

To understand best the importance of Alcott's teaching, it would be essential to experience his classroom, to observe the setting, to hear his style of questioning and the responses of his students. Fortunately, we are able to do this vicariously through the eyes and the very detailed written descriptions of Elizabeth Peabody (1969), who served as Alcott's assistant during the spring of 1836 at the Temple School in Boston. Her *Record of a School* was published later in the same year.

> The school was but one room with a large Gothic window located in the former Masonic Temple. Besides the usual desks and blackboards, large sculpture busts of Socrates, Milton, Shakespeare, and Sir Walter Scott decorated the corners of the room. (McCluskey, 1940, 85)

> And on a small bookcase two small figurines were placed, one of a child reading, and the other of a child drawing. (Peabody, 1969, 1)

Alcott's belief that art was important for the lives of his students was obvious in the appointments of his classroom as well as in his detailed curriculum plan for the week of March 1, 1836 (see Figure 4–2). His students had a weekly art class with Mr. Graeter, an art

The Tuition and Discipline are addressed in due proportion to the threefold Nature of Childhood

THE SPIRITUAL FACULTY (Means of direct Culture)	THE IMAGINATIVE FACULTY (Means of Direct Culture)	THE RATIONAL FACULTY (Means of direct Culture)
Listening to Sacred Readings Conversations on the Gospels Writing Journals Self-analysis and Self Discipline Listening to readings from works of genius Motives to study and action Government of the School	Spelling and Reading Writing and sketching from nature Picturesque geography Writing Journals and epistles Illustrating words Listening to readings Conversation	Defining Words Analyzing words Self-analysis Arithmetic Study of the Human Body Reasoning on conduct Discipline

TIME	MONDAY	TUESDAY	WEDNESDAY	THURSDAY	FRIDAY	SATURDAY
IX	Studying Spelling and Defining and Writing in Journals	Studying Geography and Sketching maps in Journals	Studying the Gospel and writing in Journals	Studying parsing lesson and writing in Journal	Paraphrasing text of reading and writing in Journals	Completing of account of weeks study in Journals
X XI	Spelling with illustrative conversations on the meaning and uses of words	Recitations in Geography with Picturesque readings and conversations	Readings and conversations on Spirit as displayed in the life of Christ	Analyzing speech written and vocal on tablets with illustrative conversations	Readings with illustrative conversations on the sense of the text	Readings from works of genius with applications and conversations
		RECREATION	ON THE COMMON	OR IN THE	ANTE-ROOM	
XII I	Studying arithmetic with demonstrations in Journals	Drawings from nature with Mr. Graeter	Conversations on the human body and its culture	Composing and writing epistles in journals	Studying arithmetic with illustrations in journals	Review of journal, Week's Conduct and Studies
		INTERMISSION	FOR REFRESHMENT	AND RECREATION		
III IV	Studying Latin and Writing in Journals	Studying Latin with Recitations	Recreation and duties at home	Studying Latin with recitations	Studying Latin and Writing in Journals	Recitations and Duties at Home

Figure 4–2

Temple School curriculum plan, March 1, 1836 (Peabody, 1969, Preface)

teacher. Under his supervision, they drew directly from nature.

The entire curriculum was designed to satisfy the "threefold nature of childhood": the spiritual faculty, the imaginative faculty, and the rational faculty. For the purpose of this book, I will concentrate on the imaginative faculty. This is where Alcott focuses primarily on writing, reading, sketching, and also geography; it is also where his unique vision and practice begin to reveal themselves. He understood that both the image and the word were essential for a good education. Peabody (1969) recalls: "A great deal of time was given to explaining the philosophy of Expression. They were taught to see that sculpture, painting, and words were only different modes of expression" (8). This insight is generally overlooked and consequently never appreciated. Notice in the curriculum plan (Figure 4–2) how he describes his subjects in "visual" terms: "picturesque" geography, "illustrating" words, "sketching" maps, "illustrative" conversations, and "picturesque" readings. This is not a clever idiosyncrasy on Alcott's part but rather a very important and accurate reflection of his unique teaching style.

Alcott had great faith in and respect for the mind of the child; in his opinion, education should be a process of "drawing out" of the child, rather than of "pouring in" (Haefner, 1937, 89). During the daily journal-writing sessions, he frequently asked his students to write about the pictures in their minds (Peabody, 1969, 29). Alcott was concerned that imaging and the cultivation of the imagination in general were vastly neglected even though the children were dependent on this faculty for reason and for judgment (McCluskey, 1940, 47–48). Elizabeth Peabody's (1969) words provide us with a glimpse of the criticism to which Alcott was subject:

> It is said that Mr. Alcott cultivates the Imagination of his scholars, inordinately, by leading them to the works of the poets and writers. It is thought, that by exercising the minds of the children in following authors of this class; requiring them to picture out all the imagery of their language; and leading them to consider, also, the inward life which this imagery is intended to symbolize, the energy of the Imagination is increased. (Preface)

Alcott took full advantage of the imaging process to inform writing—one art form informing another—and did not expect perfection in the first draft. Translating the idea was most important:

> He took the first writing (very crude) for what it was meant to be; knowing that practice would at once mend the eye and hand; but that criticism would check the desirable courage and self-confidence. (The children were very serious.) (Peabody, 1969, 6)

> Mr. Alcott said, see the advantage of having an imagination which is always ready to give the most beautiful shapes to words. It makes a great deal of difference in your characters, whether there are beautiful shapes in your characters, whether there are beautiful shapes in your minds or not; and in using words, you should take great care to use such as may put shapes into the minds of others. (Peabody, 1969, 61)

To add further insight to our understanding of Alcott's method, let us examine the visual metaphor he uses when he first explains to his class what he wants them to do:

Now, let us see if we can find the spirits of these words; if we can open the words, and bring out the thoughts and feelings. You have seen a very little seed, a mustard seed; the meaning of that seed is not felt, till it has opened out into the branches, and leaves, and fruits. (Peabody, 1969, 68–69)

He then proceeds to a lesson on the illustration of words. Peabody captures the lesson beautifully, being sensitive to Alcott's unique teaching style:

The first word to be discussed was the word *soar*. Mr. Alcott: "Our minds soar when they think on some subjects?" He asked if there were any who were conscious that their minds and hearts were beginning to aspire? One boy held up his hand. Two other boys expressed a wish that they had the eyes and wings of the eagle. Mr. Alcott said, you have stronger wings than the eagle, and eyes to see a brighter sun, than he has ever seen. Mr. Alcott then went very carefully over the process of an egg being nursed into life; the warmth of the parent bird operating upon the matter around the germ of life, and making it so pliable that the germ of life which is spirit, shapes out a form that will mean something to the observing mind. He then went over the process of a bird's learning to fly, through the encouraging love and care of the parents, animating the spirit of life and leading it out. He then asked some questions about their minds soaring out of their bodies; and some interesting answers were given. He then brought forward a cast of a child, whose arms were stretched upwards; and asked each one of them what idea this image awakened in his mind. One boy said, of a boy stretching. But almost all the boys expressed the spiritual idea of aspiration. One boy said it was an angel. (Yet there were no wings.) One girl said, it was a soul, shaped out as a child, ascending to a higher state. One boy said, it seemed to be a child looking up to Heaven, and praying to God to send an angel down to take it up

to Heaven; and that it was preparing to be received there.
(68–69)

Bronson Alcott had a wonderful ability to ask questions that stimulated the imagination of his students:

"Such of you as think you have the power of putting all you
think and feel into words, hold up your hands." Several did.
"Who say that they never yet found words that would hold all
their thoughts and feelings?" Several. "Can you understand this
definition; Imagination is the power that represents?" Yes.
"Imagination is the power by which you picture out thoughts
that never were realized in the world." (Peabody, 1969, 154–55)

Out of the mouths of his students comes the proof of his success:

Alcott: "What do you mean by Imagination?"
There were several answers, among which were the following:
"The power of conceiving thoughts in your mind, so as to see
them with your eyes."
"To see things in your mind."
"To picture forth ideas."
"To see thoughts and feelings."
"To picture forth ideas and feelings in words, which have not
come out of things."
"To picture out things in your mind a great deal more beautiful
than any in the outward world." (Peabody, 1969, 163–64)

After reflecting upon the works and the methods of Rousseau,
Froebel, and Alcott, one can only wonder how the subject of writing
was generally taught during the nineteenth century. L. A. Jackson,
in an article in *Language Arts* (1986) explains that in the nineteenth
century children wrote paraphrases of stories told orally by the teacher,
but only after the initial abilities of writing letters, words, and sentences had been developed. Jackson goes on to point out that Bronson
Alcott was a notable exception, but only because of his effective use
of journal writing, which is a popular method employed today. There
is no mention of Alcott's impressive use of visual and imaginative
stimulation, which made his teaching method unique. Jackson in-

cludes a portion of a speech given in 1892 by C. F. Adams, chairman of the Harvard Committee of Composition:

> Proficiency in athletics does not come by studying rules printed in books devoted to athletic sports or by listening to lectures on throwing curves and the like, but by practice. . . . it is only through similar, daily, and incessant practice that the degree of facility in writing the mother tongue is acquired, which always enables the student or adult to use it as a tool in his work. This is the crux of school composition. Nothing but plenty of writing, and particularly non-formal or extemporaneous writing, as in the daily work of the school under a moderate tension of criticism will transmit the pupils' specific skill into formal skill. (1986, 605)

Elliot Eisner (1981) reminds us that both visual and auditory forms of representation are essential in the cultivation of literacy. Without developing sensory skills, children are unlikely to write well, "not because they cannot spell but because they have nothing to say" (52). This could also be the case with "incessant practice."

IMPLICATIONS FOR CONTEMPORARY PRACTICE

So "why can't Johnny write?" It may often be because he is a visual learner, or at least partially so. There is a tremendous difference between visual and verbal thinking. After phonographic writing was introduced by the Greeks, it took over the way in which we see and understand reality. This takeover, as Bruno Snell (1960) points out in his study of prephonetic Minoan and postphonetic Mycenaean civilizations, determines to a very high degree what is acceptable and unacceptable about the way we view and value the world and the nature of language. Indeed, the phonetical prejudice is responsible, in large measure, for the "bad rap" so-called inferior visual thinking has (Arnheim, 1974).

The greatest discovery we can make about language, as the noted philosopher Hans-Georg Gadamer (1975) reminds us, is *not* how we "use language," but rather how language "*uses us*" (345–447). Language is not just an object or commodity for analysis and manipulation.

It is rather the preeminent mediator of meaning: it mediates not only the meaning of the world, but also the meaning of ourselves. And because our language, in its written form, is a very particular mediation in which the visual has been eliminated almost completely, Gadamer's theory helps us realize what our written language cannot give. Because of complete phonetization, it is true, as Saussure (1966) contended, that our written language provides a near perfect account of what can be *said*. But it accomplishes this at the expense of no longer providing us with a direct account of what is *seen*. Since few realize the implications of this anomaly, it is not surprising that visual thinkers, in Arnheim's (1969) phrase, should be regarded as a bit odd and even inferior to verbal thinkers.

But a great number of visual people remain. We even refer to some of the greatest people who have ever lived as "visionary." Nor have we eliminated visual metaphors such as "I see!" from our vocabularies. This book directly confronts the pedagogical and theoretical implications of the "visionary" metaphor. It is more than a mere metaphor. Buried deep within such metaphors is a residue of what is for many only a dim, partially understood, historical memory—the memory of a time when consciousness and communication were dramatically different and more visual than today. But for others—the so-called visual, nonverbal types—visual thinking is as real today as it ever was. It is their natural way of being in the world.

CHAPTER 5

REVIEW OF CURRENT EDUCATIONAL PRACTICES AFFECTING VISUAL AND VERBAL LEARNERS

Teaching strategies and curriculum decisions in art education, language arts, and special education are based on goals and beliefs. It is not readily known if these goals and beliefs are compatible or divisive, whether they have common elements or are mutually exclusive. Without this knowledge and understanding, the effect of these goals and beliefs upon the student is also unknown.

American education has gradually become very specialized, with each discipline operating quite independently from the other. Although there is a growing emphasis today regarding the need for a more encompassing liberal arts education for future teachers (Holmes Group, 1986), there is also continuing pressure to specialize in a specific area such as math, history, art, science, or music. Even if a teacher specializes in elementary education or special education, subject areas are usually addressed independently. It is generally assumed that if teachers specialize in one subject area, they will automatically understand how that subject relates to other areas. It is further assumed that they will facilitate the integration of knowledge for their students. These are very large assumptions. The responsibility for making connections between subjects is most often left to the students themselves.

In contrast, the nineteenth-century one-room schoolhouse provided the opportunity for the classroom teacher to be completely in charge of the entire school curriculum. In this instructional context, the teacher could easily integrate, correlate, and cross-reference information from all subjects and could monitor student progress over a time span of several years.

Recently, there have been numerous attempts to integrate curriculum, but generally this requires two or more teachers working closely together from their unique areas of strength. Teachers accomplish such integration either by coordinating the curriculum but working separately, or by team-teaching and actually working together in the classroom. Having experienced such teaching strategies, I know only too well that it requires a great deal more planning than when each teacher works independently. Planning sessions for cooperating teachers have to be developed, and school schedules that accommodate such collaborative efforts have to be agreed upon. Because these multiple levels of coordination and scheduling are very difficult to achieve, examples of successful collaborative efforts are few and far between.

As a consequence of these difficulties, most teachers usually proceed on very narrow paths of specialization, with the exception of most preschool and some kindergarten practitioners. During these years, the teacher, like the teacher in the one-room schoolhouse, is in control of the entire curriculum. But beginning with some kindergartens and in most first-, second-, and third-grade classrooms, teachers have very little contact with the curriculum in the "special" areas of music, art, and physical education. Indeed, these subjects are generally the first to be separated from the responsibility of the general classroom teacher. And because of this pattern of early specialization, most teachers of the lower grades are not even required to take a preparatory music or art-education course. They are instead specialists of elementary education and the teaching of so-called academic subjects—language arts, social studies, science, and math. This specialization should not, however, be confused with a college liberal arts major in English, history, natural science, or math; elementary teachers are specialists in the methods of presenting these subject areas to young children.

It is not unusual in American schools for teachers in grades four, five, and six to specialize further. I have observed many teachers in these grades who teach only one or two subjects, choosing the areas they most enjoy and within which they feel most competent. For example, if a school has two classes of fourth-grade students, one teacher may teach language arts and social studies to both classes, and the other, math and science. Beginning with seventh, eighth, and ninth grades, teachers are generally specialists in one subject and frequently have a college major in it.

With each step of specialization teachers become more limited in their understanding of other subjects and their relation to the teachers' own areas of expertise. Their understanding of students' educational development also suffers, since their observation and judgment are informed by a narrow frame of reference, both in terms of time spent with students and in terms of their disciplinary expertise.

Administrators also tend to be specialists. Directors, supervisors, and curriculum coordinators of any given subject are similarly focused on one area of study. For example, a first-grade teacher is often accountable to several administrators—the supervisor of math, of science, and so on. Even though directors are concerned with the larger curricular picture, they still operate within very narrow parameters of specialization and understanding, especially if their college degree was not a liberal arts degree.

The assumption that young children will eventually integrate information from a variety of subjects that have an apparent relationship to each other may be a gross misconception. Consider that teachers, products of this same system of education, rarely address the relationship between various subjects with their students. This could certainly be a contributing factor to the problem that this book addresses. It is a problem of very narrow vision—or no vision at all. This lack of vision has also led to a debate among educators and the public about which subjects are most important and which expendable—such judgments being informed (or misinformed, as the case may be) by the vested interests of specialists and parents alike. In other words, when education places a premium on specialization, it becomes necessary for each area, through the "every tub on its own bottom" approach, to compete for attention by convincing the powers that be of its unique contribution to the educational process. Each subject is forced to develop its own rationale regarding what is fundamental in order to make its case before administration and parents. And although each area has gone through important historical changes in this regard, I am concerned, in this book, with the goals and beliefs informing teaching strategies today and with how these strategies tend to fragment the educational process. This fragmentation is particularly destructive to visual learners, because they are the least understood in today's educational environment.

THE ART-EDUCATION PROGRAM

According to the National Art Education Association (Qualley, 1986), an effective art-education curriculum should encourage students to develop, express, and evaluate ideas. It should prompt students to produce, read, and interpret visual images, and it should lead them to recognize and understand the artistic achievements and expectations of civilized societies. As Edmund B. Feldman (1970) puts it, "Our objective [as art educators] is the development of each youngster into a fully human person" (137–38).

These goals are based on some widely held beliefs among art educators concerning the fundamental nature and purpose of art and art education. It is generally believed that art is a way of knowing and thinking about the world and our place in it, that art helps people to understand themselves and the world around them in significant and unique ways, and that children have a basic and natural desire to draw (Wilson and Wilson, 1982). Consequently, it is believed that art has value for children of all ages and should therefore be taught to all children.

It is also believed that art teaches creativity. For example, Gaitskell, Hurwitz, and Day (1982) explain that

> all children can benefit from art education because all children possess innate creative abilities that can be nurtured through art. . . . Although many aspects of life allow for creative behavior, the arts are especially appropriate for creative development because of the value placed on divergency, uniqueness, and individuality. (43)

It is further believed that art is actually a kind of language and a form of communication, that art gives form to personal ideas, feelings, and experiences that can be shared with others. This kind of visual communication also provides a unique historical and cultural record of human achievement, since the values and the beliefs of a people are manifested in the art forms that they produce. Gaitskell, Hurwitz, and Day (1982) explain that "a critical examination of these forms can lead to a better understanding of both past and present cultures" (42).

Finally, art educators believe that art contains a body of knowledge that can and should be learned by children through a carefully planned sequence of developmental activities. Gaitskell, Hurwitz, and Day (1982) contend that a meaningful school art program should include experiences in the following four areas: "Seeing and feeling visual relationships, producing works of art, knowing and understanding about art objects, and evaluating art products" (43).

The artist and the studio experience are the prevailing model for art instruction in the public school. In spite of lofty goal statements about creativity, cultural heritage, and interpretation of works of art, Brent Wilson (1988) estimates that as much as 90 percent of most curriculum guides are devoted to the development of technique rather than to issues of subject matter, symbol, or narrative. The emphasis on technique derives from the fact that art specialists in the United States have been educated as artist-teachers—that is, their primary training is in the studio. Until recently, the history of art has been considered separate from the making of art and has, therefore, rarely been taught in the public schools. The effect of the artist-teacher point of view on instructional strategies is further explained by David Baker (1987):

> In keeping with their strong convictions about the developmental nature of children, the values inherent in experimental—or hands-on learning, and the preciousness of the "unique" student-made image or object, art educators emphasize the *way* artists work and give limited curricular attention to the products of artists. Also, a pervasive and often unacknowledged belief within the field that exposure to someone else's art work will unduly inhibit a student's creativity has effectively closed art curricula to the historical study of works of art, critical discourse and aesthetic contemplations. These pedagogical beliefs have come to restrict curriculum plans to concerns about artistic techniques. Consequently, adherence to narrow developmental theories further limits the ways in which curricula is informed by the visual arts community to essentially one behavioral mode—that of the artist. (10)

THE LANGUAGE-ARTS PROGRAM

The goals of an effective language-arts program, according to the National Council of Teachers of English, are "to teach students the basic skills of listening, speaking, reading, and writing" (National Council of Teachers of English [NCTE], 1976, 1); "to teach students divergent thinking and creativity" (8); and "to help students become familiar with diverse cultures" (8).

Teaching children to read, along with the development of each child's full potential as a user of language, is generally considered the primary goal of every language-arts program (Anderson, 1972). It is also hoped that through the use of language, a love and appreciation for literature will develop (Greene and Petty, 1975).

Many language-arts teachers believe that by helping students to improve their ability to use and to respond to language creatively and responsibly, they are also encouraging them to grow as human beings. Teachers also believe that language causes students to grow emotionally and intellectually by allowing them to respond to their worlds, experiences, and feelings (NCTE, 1976).

Language-arts teachers also believe that speaking and listening help children become better readers and that telling young children stories can motivate them to read. Story telling is viewed as an important way to introduce children to cultural values and literary traditions before they themselves have the ability to read and to write (Burns, Broman, and Wantling, 1971; Anderson, 1972). It is also commonly believed that drawing is a useful method to motivate story telling for kindergarten and first-grade students. Drawing in the upper grades, however, is thought to interfere with the writing process and should therefore be discouraged (Calkins, 1986, 69).

It is commonly believed that children possess a natural desire to write (Calkins, 1986), that writing is central to thinking and learning for all children in all content areas, and that language is humanity's unique way of creating meaning from what is observed and/or experienced (Brookline Public Schools, 1986). These beliefs contribute to the notion that only words have the capacity to express thoughts and that verbal language is the basis of all communication (Anderson, 1972; Greene and Petty, 1975).

Educators further contend that language is indeed the most important tool ever invented, because it is the primary means by which one explores and structures one's world; it enables human beings to transmit their heritage and culture from one generation to another. Greene and Petty (1975) elaborate:

> Mankind has accomplished nothing more wonderful than the development of language. Through language, feelings and thoughts are made known; through language, actions and reactions are stimulated; language is basic for acquiring most understandings, attitudes, and ideals. Language is a part of mankind. It is fundamental in solving problems, gaining inspiration, and securing emotional release. It is an integral part of a culture. It makes possible a society. (1)

Thus language, in its ordinary sense, is commonly believed to be the sole vehicle of teaching and learning (Burns, Broman, and Wantling, 1971; Anderson 1972).

The most effective way to teach reading and writing has long been a subject for debate among language-arts teachers. Some advocate the teaching of phonics; others promote the whole-language approach (Chall, 1967; Newman, 1985; Pflaum, 1986). The phonics approach stresses the relationship between letters and sounds and "breaking the code" that links the words children hear with the words they see in print. Good phonics strategies include teaching children the sounds of letters in isolation as well as in words and the ways to blend the sounds together. The whole-language approach stresses the understanding of the meaning of the "whole" (that is, an entire sentence, paragraph, or text) rather than the accurate identification of every word. New words are often learned in context, rather than individually. Students learn that the meaning of the whole isn't dependent on being able to identify every word. Students are encouraged to predict, confirm, integrate information from the whole. Those who advocate the phonics approach usually prefer the use of basal readers, and they often emphasize correct grammar and spelling before wrestling with ideas. Those who advocate the whole-language approach often prefer literature and encourage invented spelling in order not to lose an idea, saving corrections for a later step (Newman, 1985).

Many language-arts teachers today believe the most effective way to teach writing is by the "process" of brainstorming, composing, revising, and editing (Graves, 1983; Calkins, 1986). This method uses the professional writer as a model. More traditional teachers favor a greater emphasis on the mechanics of writing. Donald Murray (1984/85) has argued that language-arts programs too often emphasize the techniques of writing rather than thinking:

> Schools focus too much on handwriting, spelling, usage, mechanics. These are relatively small matters that can—and should—be mopped up on the final draft. Emphasizing them has, in many school systems, made writing trivial and eliminated instruction that allows students to learn that writing is thinking. (55)

THE SPECIAL-EDUCATION PROGRAM
FOR THE LEARNING DISABLED

The primary goals of special-education programs for students with learning disabilities are to identify the problem, to pinpoint its cause, and finally, to correct it with effective methods of instruction (Torgesen and Wong, 1986).

It is commonly believed that if a student has difficulty learning to read or to write by traditional teaching methods, that student must obviously be "learning disabled." It is also believed that a learning disability is a language-related disorder caused by a neurological problem in otherwise normal children, of average to superior intelligence, living in normal environmental conditions and having adequate learning opportunities (Coles, 1987, 12). Most special-education teachers and parents believe that something must be "wrong" with these children—possibly defective brain tissue, a malfunctioning brain area, or simply a bad gene. There appears to be complete faith in the physical sciences to provide the answer so that the problem can be "fixed" (Bannatyne, 1971; Torgesen and Wong, 1986).

Students with learning disabilities are generally regarded as presenting an educational challenge that initially is best served by a series of special tests and evaluations. Such students are referred to the Special Education Department. An educational plan is then devised. These plans and methods do not seem to be significantly different from those for so-called normal students, however, other than that they recommend more individual attention and a slower pace of instruction.

The use of computers as an instructional tool for the learning disabled and for "normal" students has increased dramatically in recent years. Computers are particularly useful for students who have difficulty with the actual act of writing (Torgesen and Wong, 1986, chap. 14). Thus the computer is an extremely beneficial adaptive tool, assisting the student with the mechanics and the physical act of writing. This is an important feature, but the computer is limited in its ability to serve the needs of the visual learner. It cannot magically cause students to be more insightful or thoughtful writers. It cannot magically translate what is observed and experienced into content. The computer is not a substitute for creativity.

conclusion

Very few art teachers or English teachers are aware of the strong similarities between their respective subjects. Each area is said to be a form of communication and a way of thinking—a primary means of knowing, experiencing, and understanding the world; teachers in each area claim to be teaching creativity and transmitting a historical and cultural record of human achievement; and each teacher claims that children have a natural desire to draw (Wilson and Wilson, 1982) or to write (Calkins, 1986).

An interesting twist in instructional strategies is taking place, however. Language-arts programs have traditionally emphasized the reading of good literature as examples of writing to be emulated, and art programs have stressed the processes of making art with the artist as model. Although language-arts programs have also stressed the mechanics of writing, including the parts of speech and correct spelling, art programs have emphasized self-expression. More recently, however, there has been an inversion of methodological emphasis in these two fields. Art education is beginning to stress a more academic approach to the understanding of art, using the visual elements and the principles of design as prerequisites for making and understanding art, and de-emphasizing the making of art objects in favor of art history, criticism, and aesthetics. Language-arts programs, on the other hand, are stressing more self-expression and the process approach to writing with the writer as model. Thus we have a rather odd situation in which two disciplines seem to be exchanging instructional strategies at the same time. If the instructional methodologies of these two fields were more effectively shared and compared, however, these disciplines might mutually benefit—the left hand might learn from the right, so to speak. In short, if the educational goals, beliefs, and instructional strategies for teaching visual and verbal expression were viewed as being complementary rather than different, and mutually supportive rather than competitive, the learner could benefit a great deal. But with art education presently striving toward a more verbal

155

approach, with language arts continuing to ignore the visual component in verbal expression even though they are putting greater emphasis on the writing process, and with special education continuing its effort to "fix" what must be "wrong," the needs of the visual learner will continue to be misunderstood and inadequately served by our school systems. Until these deficiencies are remedied, visual learners will have little opportunity to reach their full educational potential.

This book began with the observation that children's drawings have a narrative dimension; that is, children like to tell stories with their drawings. But contrary to the notion that this is merely a preliterate tendency, something to be gradually if not totally displaced by writing as children improve their language skills, this book has tried to demonstrate the interactive continuity of visual and verbal modes of expression and the benefits their integration could have for visual children/ reluctant writers and all other children.

By developing an art program based on visual-narrative drawing, we soon saw that the visual and verbal modes of expression are indeed compatible and share many elements. Thus, by formulating and implementing strategies whereby the visual and verbal modes of expression can be integrated, by "envisioning writing," so to speak, I have shown through numerous examples that students will, in most cases, manifest marked and often dramatic improvements in their writing skills.

I have also addressed the problem of specialization in the public schools—specialization that sometimes stands in the way of implementing an interdisciplinary program such as this. Specialization and the fragmentation to which it may lead can contribute to highly narrow views regarding the aptitudes and competencies of students, particularly those students who are primarily visual learners. Such views tend to be both mirrored in and reinforced by curriculum structures that militate against interactive modes of developing verbal and visual literacy.

I stress, therefore, the need for basic changes in instructional theory by indicating how the visual learner functions; I also suggest changes in practice by providing examples as to how revisions in theory can be implemented. Such changes are particularly urgent in the areas of art, language arts, and special education in order to serve *all* students better.

works cited

Anderson, P. S. (1972). *Language skills in elementary education* (2nd ed.). New York: Macmillan.

Arnheim, R. (1969). *Visual thinking.* Berkeley, CA: University of California Press.

Arnheim, R. (1974). *Art and visual perception.* Berkeley, CA: University of California Press.

Arrowsmith, N. (1977). *A field guide to the little people.* New York: Pocket Books.

Baker, D. W. (1987). *Artist-teachers: A concept in question.* Unpublished manuscript contracted by the Alliance for the Independent Colleges of Art.

Bannatyne, A. (1971). *Language, reading and learning disabilities.* Springfield, IL: Charles C. Thomas.

Bettelheim, B. (1977). *The uses of enchantment.* New York: Vintage.

Brookline Public Schools (1986). *Brookline writing manual.* Brookline, MA.

Bruner, J. (1986). *Actual minds, possible worlds.* Cambridge, MA: Harvard University Press.

Burns, P. C., Broman, B. & Wantling, A. (1971). *The language arts in childhood education* (2nd ed.). Chicago: Rand McNally.

Burton, J. (1980, October). The first visual symbols. *School Arts,* pp. 60–65.

Calkins, L. M. (1986). *The art of teaching writing.* Portsmouth, NH: Heinemann.

Carroll, J. B., & Chall, J. S. (1975). *Toward a literate society.* New York: McGraw-Hill.

Chall, J. S. (1967). *Learning to read: the great debate.* New York: McGraw-Hill.

Coles, G. (1987). *The learning mystique: A critical look at "learning disabilities."* New York: Pantheon.

Dixon, J. P. (1983). *The spatial child.* Springfield, IL: Charles C. Thomas.

Einstein, A. (1976). *Ideas and opinions.* New York: Dell.

Eisner, E. W. (1981, September). The role of the arts in cognition and curriculum. *Phi Delta Kappan,* 48–52.

Fazzioli, E. (1987). *Chinese calligraphy.* New York: Abbeville Press.

Feldman, E. B. (1970). *Becoming human through art.* Englewood Cliffs, NJ: Prentice Hall.

Feldman, E. B. (1971). The art of curriculum making in the arts. In E. W. Eisner

(Ed.), *Confronting curriculum reform* (pp. 112–19). Boston: Little, Brown.

Feldman, E. B. (1981). *Varieties of visual experience.* Englewood Cliffs, NJ: Prentice Hall.

Flesch, R. (1955). *Why Johnny can't read.* New York: Harper.

Flesch, R. (1981). *Why Johnny still can't read.* New York: Harper.

Froebel, F. (1974). *The education of man* (W. N. Hailman, Trans.). Clifton, NJ: Augustus M. Kelley. (Original work published 1826, published in English 1887.)

Froud, B., and Lee, A. (1978). *Faeries.* New York: Harry Abrams.

Gadamer, H. (1975). *Truth and method.* New York: Seabury.

Gardner, H. (1982). *Art, mind and brain.* New York: Basic Books.

Gaitskell, C. D., Hurwitz, A., and Day, M. (1982). *Children and their art.* New York: Harcourt Brace Jovanovich.

Gelb, I. M. (1952). *A study of writing: Foundations of grammatology.* Chicago: University of Chicago Press.

Graves, D. H. (1983). *Writing: Teachers and children at work.* Portsmouth, NH: Heinemann.

Greene, H., & Petty, W. (1975). *Developing language skills in the elementary schools* (5th ed.). Boston: Allyn & Bacon.

Haefner, G. E. (1937). *A critical estimate of the education theories and practices of A. Bronson Alcott.* Westport, CT: Greenwood Press.

Havelock, E. (1976). *The origins of western literacy.* Toronto: University of Toronto Press.

Holmes Group. (1986). *Tomorrow's teachers.* East Lansing, MI: Holmes Group.

Hook, J. N. (1986, October). NCTC and elementary teachers. *Language arts*, pp. 538–543.

Jackson, L. A. (1986, October). Nineteenth-century elementary composition instruction. *Language Arts*, pp. 601–06.

John-Steiner, V. (1985). *Notebooks of the mind.* Albuquerque: University of New Mexico Press.

Kavanagh, J. F., & Mattingly, I. G. (Eds.). (1972). *Language by ear and by eye.* Cambridge, MA: MIT Press.

Langer, S. (1942). *Philosophy in a new key.* Cambridge, MA: Harvard University Press.

Lilley, I. M. (1967). *Friedrich Froebel.* Cambridge, MA: Harvard University Press.

Long, J. (1987). *The art of Chinese calligraphy.* New York: Blandford Press.

McCluskey, D. (1940). *Bronson Alcott, Teacher.* New York: Arno.

McGuinness, D. (1985). *When children don't learn: Understanding the biology and psychology of learning disabilities.* New York: Basic Books.

Mitchell, W. J. T. (Ed.). (1980). *The language of images.* Chicago: University of Chicago Press.

Moffet, J. (1968). *A student-centered language arts curriculum.* Boston: Houghton Mifflin.

Morse, J. D. (Ed.). (1972). *Ben Shahn.* New York: Praeger.

Murray, D. (1984/85). On the cutting edge: Writing. *Today's Education.* pp. 54–5.

National Council of Teachers of English. (1976). *A statement on the preparation of teachers of English and the language arts.* Urbana, IL: National Council of Teachers of English.

Newman, J. M. (Ed.). (1985). *Whole language: Theory in use.* Portsmouth, NH: Heinemann.

Olson, J. (1982, November). Think of the possibilities. *School Arts*, pp. 31–35.

Olson, J., & Wilson, B. (1979, September). A visual narrative program—grades 1–8. *School Arts*, pp. 26–33.

Peabody, E. P. (1969). *Record of a school: Exemplifying the general principles of spiritual culture.* Boston: Russell, Shattuck & Co. (Original work published 1836.)

Pflaum, S. W. (1986). *The development of language and literacy in young children.* Columbus, OH: Charles E. Merrill.

Qualley, C. A. (1986). *Quality art education.* Reston, VA: National Art Education Association.

Rousseau, J. J. (1984). *Emile* (B. Foxley, Trans.). London: Everyman's Library. (Original work published 1762)

Sattler, J. M. (1982). *Assessment of children's intelligence and special abilities.* Boston: Allyn and Bacon.

Saussure, F. de (1966). *Course in general linguistics.* New York: McGraw-Hill.

Sendak, M. (1963). *Where the wild things are.* New York: Harper.

Snell, B. (1960). *The discovery of the mind.* New York: Harper and Row.

Taylor, G. R. (1979). *The natural history of the mind.* New York: Penguin.

Teachers College. (February, 1987). *Learning disabled children can write.* Conference sponsored by the Department of Special Education and the Child Study Center, Columbia University, New York.

Tedlock, D. (1981). Between text and interpretation: The anthropologist and the alphabet. In J. Ruby (Ed.), *A crack in the mirror: Reflective perspectives in anthropology* (pp. 268–89). Philadelphia: University of Pennsylvania Press.

Torgesen, J. K., & Wong, Y. L. (Eds.). (1986). *Psychological and educational perspec-*

tives on learning disabilities. New York: Academic Press.

Updike, J. (1963). *The dogwood tree.* New York: Knopf.

Vygotsky, L. S. (1978). *Mind in society.* Cambridge, MA: Harvard University Press.

Weigl, E. (1980, March). The written language is more than reading and writing. *Reading Teacher*, pp. 652–57.

Wilson, B. (1988). *Art education, civilization and the 21st century: A researcher's reflections on the National Endowment for the Arts report to Congress.* Reston, VA: National Art Education Association.

Wilson, B., Hurwitz, A., & Wilson, M. (1987). *Teaching drawing from art.* Worcester, MA: Davis.

Wilson, B., & Wilson, M. (1979, April). Children's story drawing: Reinventing worlds. *School Arts*, pp. 6–11.

Wilson, B., & Wilson, M. (1982). *Teaching children to draw.* Englewood Cliffs, Prentice Hall.

Ysseldyke, J. E., & Algozzine. (1984). *Introduction to special education.* Boston: Houghton Mifflin.

suggested reading

Ames, L. B. (1983). Learning disability: truth or trap? *Journal of Learning Disabilities, 16*(1), 14–20.

Applebee, A. N. (1978). *The child's concept of story.* Chicago: University of Chicago Press.

Applebee, A. N., Langer, J. A. & Mullis, V. S. (1985). *Writing: Trends across the decade, 1974–84.* Princeton, NJ: Educational Testing Service.

Arnheim, R. (1979). A plea for visual thinking. In W. J. T. Mitchell (Ed.), *The language of images*, (pp. 171–80). Chicago: University of Chicago Press.

Arnheim, R. (1979). Visual thinking in education. In A. A. Sheikh & J. T. Shaffer (Eds.), *The potential of fantasy and imagination* (pp. 215–25). New York: Brandon House.

Atwell, N., & Newkirk, T. (Eds.). (1980). *Understanding writing: Ways of observing, learning and teaching K-8.* Cambridge, MA: Harvard University Press.

Baker, D. W. (1982). *Rousseau's children: A historical analysis of the romantic paradigm in art education.* Unpublished doctoral dissertation, Pennsylvania State University.

Baker, D. W. (1991). What is art education for? In K. Carroll (Ed.), *What is art for?* (pp. 5–13). Reston, VA: National Art Education Association.

Barthes, R. (1972). *Mythologies.* New York: Hill and Wang.

Bennett, W. J. (1986). *First lessons.* Washington, D.C.: U.S. Government Printing Office.

Bennett, W. J. (1986). *What works.* Washington, D.C.: U.S. Department of Education.

Bettelheim, B., & Zelan, K. (1982). *On learning to read.* New York: Knopf.

Bloom, L. (1980). Language development, language disorders, and learning disabilities: LD. *Bulletin of the Orton Society, 30*, 115–133.

Brainerd, C. J., & Pressly, M. (Eds.). (1982). *Verbal processes in children.* New York: Springer.

Britton, J. (1983). Writing and the story world. In B. M. Kroll & G. Wells (Eds.), *Explorations in the development of writing* (pp. 3–30). New York: John Wiley & Sons.

Bruner, J. (1979). *On knowing.* Cambridge, MA: Harvard University Press.

Bryson, N. (1986). *Word and image.* London: Cambridge University Press.

Burton, J. (1980, September). Beginnings of artistic language. *School Arts*, pp. 6–12.

Burton, J. (1980, November). Visual events. *School Arts*, pp. 58–64.

Burton, J. (1980, December). Representing experience from imagination and observation. *School Arts*, pp. 26–30.

Burton. J. (1981, January). Representing experiences: ideas in search of forms. *Schools Arts*, pp. 58–64.

Carroll, J. B. (1974). *Language, thought and reality from selected writings of Benjamin Lee Whorf.* Cambridge, MA: MIT Press.

Chomsky, C. (1979). *The acquisition of syntax in children from 5 to 10.* Cambridge, MA: MIT Press.

Cleator, P. E. (1961). *Lost languages.* New York: John Day.

Cooper, D. E. (1973). *Philosophy and the nature of language.* London: Longman.

Copperman, P. (1978). *The literacy hoax: The decline of reading, writing and learning in the public schools and what we can do about it.* New York: William Morrow.

Derrida, J. (1974). *Of grammatology* (G. C. Spivak, Trans.). Baltimore: John Hopkins University Press.

Dewey, J. (1980). *Art as experience.* New York: G. P. Putnam. (Original work published 1934.)

Dobbs, S. M. (Ed.). (1983). Art and the mind [Special issue]. *Art Education, 36* (2).

Donaldson, M. (1979). *Children's minds.* New York: Norton.

Dyson, A. H. (1986). Transitions and tensions: Interrelationships between the drawing, talking, and dictating of young children. *Research in the Teaching of English, 20* (4), 379–409.

Ehrenzweig, A. (1965). *The psychoanalysis of artistic vision and hearing.* London: Sheldon Press.

Eisner, E. W. (1972). *Educating artistic vision.* New York: Macmillan.

Eisner, E. W. (1978, May). The impoverished mind. *Educational Leadership, 9,* 615–23.

Eisner, E. W. (Ed.). (1978). *Reading, the arts, and the creation of meaning.* Reston, VA: National Art Education Association.

Elbow, P. (1981). *Writing with power: Techniques for mastering the writing process.* New York: Oxford University Press.

Emler, N. P. & Heather, N. (1980). Intelligence: An ideological bias of conventional psychology. In P. Salmon (Ed.), *Coming to know* (pp. 135–51). London: Routledge & Kegan Paul.

Evertts, E. (Ed.). (1970). *Explorations in children's writing.* Champaign, IL: National Council of Teachers of English.

Fadely, J. L., & Hosler, V. N. (1979). *Understanding the alpha child.* Springfield, IL: Charles C. Thomas.

Farnham-Diggory, S. (1978). *Learning disabilities.* Cambridge, MA: Harvard University Press.

Gardner, H. (1973). *The arts and human development.* New York: Wiley.

Gardner, H. (1981). *Artful scribbles.* New York: Basic Books.

Gardner, H. (1983). *Frames of mind.* New York: Basic Books.

Ghiselin, B. (Ed.). (1952). *The creative process.* New York: Signet.

Giedion, S. (1962). *The eternal present: The beginnings of art.* New York: Random House.

Golomb, C. (1974). *Young children's sculpture and drawing.* Cambridge, MA: Harvard University Press.

Goodenough, F. (1926). *Measurement of intelligence by drawings.* New York: World Book.

Goodman, N. (1976). *Languages of art.* Indianapolis: Hackett.

Goodman, N. (1978). *Ways of worldmaking.* Indianapolis: Hackett.

Goodnow, J. (1977). *Children drawing.* Cambridge, MA: Harvard University Press.

Gordon, C. H. (1968). *Forgotten scripts.* New York: Basic Books.

Gordon, N. (Ed.). (1984). *Classroom experiences: The writing process in action.* Portsmouth, NH: Heinemann.

Graham, S. & Harris, K. R. (Eds.). (1988). Research and instruction in written language [Special issue]. *Exceptional Children, 54*(6).

Hammill, D. D., Leigh, J. E., McNutt, G. & Larsen, S. C. (1987). A new definition of learning disabilities. *Journal of Learning Disabilities, 20*(2), 109–113.

Hardiman, G. W., & Zernich, T. (Eds.). (1981). *Foundations for curriculum development and evaluation in art education.* Champaign, IL: Stipes Publishing.

Harrison, A. (1978). *Making and thinking: A study of intelligent activities.* Indianapolis: Hackett.

Hjerter, K. G. (1986). *Doubly gifted: The author as visual artist.* New York: Harry N. Abrams.

Hubbard, R. (1987, January). Transferring images: Not just glued on the page. *Young Children,* pp. 60–67.

Hubbard, R. (1989). *Authors of pictures, draughtsmen of words.* Portsmouth, NH: Heinemann.

Hurwitz, A. (Ed.). (1983). *Drawing for the schools: A conference.* Baltimore: Maryland Institute, College of Art.

Hymes, D. (1964). *Language in culture and society: A reader in linguistics and anthropology*. New York: Harper.

Jensen, H. (1969). *Sign, symbol and script*. New York: Putnam.

Jespersen, O. (1964). *Language: Its nature, development and origin*. New York: Norton.

Kaufman, I. (1985). *Art and education in contemporary culture*. New York: Macmillan.

Kellogg, R. (1959). *What children scribble and why*. San Francisco: N-P Publishers.

Klee, F. (Ed.). (1964). *The diaries of Paul Klee 1898–1918*. Berkeley: University of California Press.

Kroll, B. M., & Wells, G. (Eds.). (1983). *Explorations in the development of writing*. New York: John Wiley and Sons.

Lamb, P. (1967). *Guiding children's language learning*. Dubuque: Brown and Company.

Langer, S. (1957). *Problems of art*. New York: Scribner's.

Lapate, P. (1975). *Being with children*. New York: Doubleday.

Lapp, D., & Flood, J. (1978). *Teaching reading to every child*. New York: Macmillan.

Levick, M. F. (1983). *They could not talk and so they drew: Children's styles of coping and thinking*. Springfield, IL: Charles C. Thomas.

Levin, J. R., Divine-Hawkins, P., Kerst, S. M., & Guttmann, J. (1974). Individual differences in learning from pictures and words: The development and application of an instrument. *Journal of Educational Psychology, 66* (3), 296–303.

Lindauer, M. S. (1983). Imagery and the arts. In A. A. Sheikh (ed.), *Imagery: Current theory, research, and application* (pp. 468–506). New York: John Wiley & Sons.

Logan, R. K. (1986). *The alphabet effect: The impact of the phonetic alphabet on the development of western civilization*. New York: William Morrow.

Lowenfeld, V. (1957). *Creative and mental growth*. New York: Macmillan.

Mangieri, J. N., Staley, N. K. & Wilhide, J. A. (1984). *Teaching language arts*. New York: McGraw-Hill.

Mann, L., Davis, C. H., Boyer, C. W., Metz, C. M., & Wolford, B. (1983). LD or not LD, that was the question: A retrospective analysis of child service demonstration centers' compliance with the federal definition of learning disabilities. *Journal of Learning Disabilities, 16*(1), 14–17.

Mattil, E. L. (Ed.). (1966). *A seminar in art education for research and curriculum development*. University Park, PA: Pennsylvania State University Press.

May, F. (1967). *Teaching language as communication to children*. Columbus, OH: Merrill.

Merleau-Ponty, M. (1964). *The primacy of perception*. Chicago: Northwestern University Press.

Merleau-Ponty, M. (1968). *The visible and the invisible.* Chicago: Northwestern University Press.

Miller, G. (1973). *Communication, language and meaning.* New York: Basic Books.

Mitchell, W. J. T. (1986). *Iconology: Image, text, ideology.* Chicago: University of Chicago Press.

Moffet, J. (1981). *Active voice: A writing program across the curriculum.* Portsmouth, NH: Boynton/Cook.

Mulholland, T. (1978). A program for the EEG study of attention in visual communication. In B. Randhawa & W. E. Coffman (Eds.), *Visual learning, thinking, and communication* (pp. 77–91).

Murray, D. (1984). *Write to learn.* New York: Holt, Rinehart & Winston.

National Endowment for the Arts (1988). *Toward civilization: A report on arts education.* Washington, D.C.: National Endowment for the Arts.

National Joint Committee on Learning Disabilities. (1987, February). Learning disabilities: Issues on definition. *Journal of learning disabilities, 20(2)*, 107–8.

Nodine, B. F., Barenbaum, E., & Newcomer, P. (1985). Story composition by learning disabled, reading disabled, and normal children. *Learning Disability Quarterly, 8* (Summer), 167–79.

Olson, J. (1987, September). Drawing to write. *School Arts*, pp. 25–27.

Olson, J., Prager, M., & Henry, E. J. (1986, February). Fantastic vehicles. *School Arts*, pp. 27–29.

Oppenheimer, H. (1986), *Lorca: The drawings.* New York: Franklin Watts.

Ornstein, R. (1972). *The psychology of consciousness.* New York: Penguin.

Paivio, A. (1971). *Imagery and verbal processes.* New York: Holt, Rinehart and Winston.

Pappas, G. (Ed.). (1970). *Concepts in art and education.* New York: Macmillan.

Parker, F. W. (1969). *Talks on pedagogics.* New York: Arno. (Original work published 1894.)

Piaget, J. (1955). *The language and thought of the child.* New York: Meridian.

Piaget, J., and Inhelder, B. (1964). *The early growth of logic in the child.* London: Routledge and Kegan Paul.

Piaget, J., and Inhelder, B. (1969). *The psychology of the child.* New York: Basic Books.

Propp, V. (1968). *Morphology of the folktale.* Austin: University of Texas Press.

Quakenbos, G. P. (1851). *First lessons in composition.* New York: American Book.

Randhawa, B. & Coffman, W. E. (Eds.). (1978). *Visual learning, thinking, and communication.* New York: Academic Press.

Read, H. (1956). *Education through art.* New York: Pantheon.

Read, H. (1982). *The meaning of art.* London: Faber and Faber.

Richardson, J. T. E. (1983). Mental imagery in thinking and problem solving. In J. Evans (Ed.), *Thinking and reasoning* (pp. 197–226). London: Routledge & Kegan Paul.

Rickoff, A. J. (1877). *A reply to our common school education.* Cleveland, OH: Leader Printing Company.

Ricoeur, P. (1975). *Interpretation theory: Discourse and the surplus of meaning.* Fort Worth: Texas Christian University.

Ricoeur, P. (1975). *The rule of metaphor.* Toronto: University of Toronto Press.

Riemer, G. (1969). *How they murdered the second R.* New York: Norton.

Root-Bernstein, R. S. (1985). Visual thinking: The art of imagining reality. *Transactions of the American Philosophical Society, 75* (6), 50–67.

Root-Bernstein, R. S. (1987). Education and the fine arts from a scientist's perspective: A challenge. A "White Paper" written for the College of Fine Arts, U.C.L.A.

Rousseau, J. J. & Herder, J. G. (1966). *On the origin of language.* Chicago: University of Chicago Press.

Sacks, S. (Ed.). (1979). *On metaphor.* Chicago: University of Chicago Press.

Salmon, P. (Ed.). (1980). *Coming to know.* London: Routledge & Kegan Paul.

Scholes, R., and Kellog, R. (1966). *The nature of narrative.* New York: Oxford University Press.

Selfe, Lorna. (1977). *Nadia: The case of extraordinary drawing ability in an autistic child.* New York: Harcourt Brace Jovanovich.

Shahn, B. (1957). *The shape of content.* Cambridge, MA: Harvard University Press.

Shapard, R. N. (1978). Externalization of mental images and the act of creation. In B. S. Randhawa and W. E. Coffman (Eds.), *Visual learning, thinking, and communication* (pp. 133–89). New York: Harcourt Brace Jovanovich.

Sheikh, A. A., & Shaffer, J. T. (Eds.). (1979). *The potential of fantasy and imagination.* New York: Brandon House.

Sheldon, E. A. (1873). *A manuel of elementary instruction.* New York: Scribner, Armstrong and Company.

Shepherd, M. J. (1989). Developmental reading disorder. In H. Kaplan & B. J. Sadock, (Eds.), *The comprehensive textbook of psychiatry* (5th ed.). Baltimore: Williams & Wilkins.

Shepherd, M. J. (1989). Developmental reading disorder. In H. Kaplan & B. J. Sadock (Eds.), *The comprehensive textbook of psychiatry* (5th ed.). Baltimore: Williams & Wilkins.

Shepherd, M. J. (1989). Expressive writing disorder. In H. Kaplan & B. J. Sadock

Sinatra, R. (1986). *Visual literacy connections to thinking, reading and writing.* Springield, IL: Charles C. Thomas.

Smith, S. L. (1978). *No easy answers: The learning disabled child.* Washington, D.C.: U. S. Department of Health, Education, and Welfare.

Spalding, W., & Spalding, R. B. (1962). *The writing road to reading.* New York: Morrow.

Speidel, G. E., & Pickens, A. L. (1979). Art, mental imagery, and cognition. In A. A. Sheikh & J. T. Shaffer (Eds.), *The potential of fantasy and imagination* (pp. 199–213). New York: Brandon House.

Springer, N. (1974). *The natural way to read.* Boston: Little, Brown.

Stewig, J. W. (1975). *Read to write.* New York: 1975.

Stewig. J. W. (1982). *Teaching language arts in early childhood.* New York: Holt, Rinehart and Winston.

Straus, E. (1963). *The primary world of the senses.* London: Collier-Macmillan.

Strickland, R. (1969). *The language arts in the elementary school.* Lexington, MA: Heath.

Strickland, D. S., and Morrow, L. M. (Eds.). (1989). *Emerging literacy: Young children learn to read and write.* Newark, Delaware: IRA.

Tedlock, D. (1979, August), Beyond logocentrism: Trace and voice among the Quiché Maya. *Boundary 2,* pp. 321–33.

Temple, C. A., Nathan, R. G., & Burris, N. A. (1982). *The beginnings of writing.* Boston: Allyn & Bacon.

Tidyman, W., and Weddle, C. (1969). *Teaching the language arts.* New York: McGraw-Hill.

Torjusen, Bente. (1986). *Words and images of Edvard Munch.* Chelsea, VT: Chelsea Green Publishing Company.

Traditional Chinese culture in R. O. C. on Taiwan. (1986). Heritage series 2 (3rd ed.). Taiwan: Kwang Hwa Publishing Company.

Villiers, P. A. de, & Villiers, J. G. de. (1979). *Early language.* Cambridge, MA: Harvard University Press.

Vygotsky, L. S. (1962). *Thought and language.* (E. Hanfmann & G. Vakar, Trans.). Cambridge, MA: MIT Press. (Original work published 1934)

Vygotsky, L. S. (1971). *The psychology of art.* Cambridge, MA: MIT Press.

Wallach, M. A., & Kogan, N. (1965). *Modes of thinking in young children.* New York: Holt Rinehart & Winston.

West, F. (1975). *The way of language.* New York: Harcourt Brace Jovanovich.

Wiener, H. (1978). *Any child can write.* New York: McGraw-Hill.

Williams, R. M. (1977, September 3). Why children should draw: The surprising link between art and learning. *Saturday Review*, p. 16.

Wilson, B., & Wilson, M. (1979, May). Drawing realities: The themes of children's story drawings. *School Arts*, pp. 12–17.

Wilson, B., & Wilson, M. (1979, June). Of graphic vocabularies and grammars: Teaching drawing skills for worldmaking. *School Arts*, pp. 36–41.

Wilson, B., & Wilson, M. (1979, October). I draw—you draw: The graphic dialogue. *School Arts*, pp. 50–55.

Wilson, B., & Wilson, M. (1979, November). The extended graphic dialogue. *School Arts*, pp. 37–41.

Winner, E. (1982). *Invented worlds*. Cambridge, MA: Harvard University Press.

Wollheim, R. (1974). *On art and the mind*. Cambridge, MA: Harvard University Press.

Wygant, F. (1983). *Art in american schools in the nineteenth century*. Cincinnati: Interwood Press.

index